D0923534

The Land That Never Melts

The Land That Never Melts
Auyuittuq National Park

edited by Roger Wilson

Peter Martin Associates Limited
in association with

 Indian and   Affaires
Northern   indiennes
Affairs   et du Nord

Parks Canada   Parcs Canada

and Publishing Centre, Supply and Services Canada

Canadian Cataloguing in Publication Data

Main entry under title:

The Land that never melts

ISBN 0-88778-143-8 bd.   ISBN 0-88778-144-6 pa.

1. Auyuittuq National Park, N.W.T.
I. Wilson, Roger, 1942-   II. Canada. Parks Canada.

FC4164.A88L35   917.195   C76-017087-8
F1105.B3L35

Design: Diana McElroy, Tim Wynne-Jones

PETER MARTIN ASSOCIATES
35 Britain Street, Toronto, Canada M5A 1R7

United Kingdom: Books Canada, 1 Bedford Road, London N2, England.
United States: Books Canada, 33 East Tupper St., Buffalo, N.Y. 14203.

Contents

Introduction

In a world in which "frontiers" are vanishing and wildlands are at a premium, we are fortunate to have the north. Still relatively untouched and representing one of Canada's great natural resources, it has played a considerable, though often indirect, role in shaping our society. If there indeed exists that hazy and often-referred-to "Canadian identity", it should be credited as much to our northern wilderness as to any other factor.

Over the past 300 years northern Canada has challenged and inspired writers, artists and explorers. Traders, whalers, missionaries and various governments have brought enormous and rapid changes to its native people. In the search for oil and mineral wealth, parts of this frontier have been pushed back against odds once viewed as too high to justify the risk.

This recently accelerated interest in northern resources and a growing concern for the northern environment have resulted in an explosion of information. Our awareness has been heightened by magazine and newspaper articles, television programs, scientific reports and native land claims. Yet this territory is so vast that it remains for many of us a mysterious and poorly understood land.

This mystery has probably contributed greatly to the fact that growing numbers of people are visiting the north to experience it firsthand. It was the recognition of this increased interest in the north, ever greater expanses of which are being demanded for resource exploration, and of the need for northern landscapes in our national park system that accelerated the search by park planners for northern areas suitable for national park status. In 1972 this search was rewarded by the establishment of three national parks. The most northerly of these was Auyuittuq National Park, "the land that never melts" and the subject of this book.

How can one completely describe, in a handbook of this size, such a spectacular landscape? It isn't possible. What we have tried to do instead is to provide some of the basics necessary to the understanding of Auyuittuq.

Our perception of these "basics" is responsible for the order in which the various subjects have been treated. In order to understand any landscape, some knowledge is required of the shape of the land, the processes that molded it and continue to shape it, and the constraints and benefits imposed by climate on both the non-living and living parts of the landscape.

Man in the landscape seemed to us to be next in the scheme of things. When we realize that the ancestors of the present-day Inuit had adapted to life in this harsh environment at about the time the pyramids were being built and some 3,000 years before the first Europeans saw the New World we begin to gain a perspective on the arctic environment and man's place in it.

A study of how man has adapted to life in the north leads naturally to a consideration of northern ecosystems and the surprising variety of life to be found in the Arctic. The discussion of northern ecology in general and the specific sections on plants, birds and mammals which follow are meant to indicate the interrelation of landform, climate and living things. These three elements, in fact, are really what "landscape" is all about.

So much for Auyuittuq as a landscape. Now, what about you as a visitor to this area? The last chapter in this book is intended to be of help to those who will venture into this arctic national park.

You must be prepared to take the north on its own terms. A trip to Auyuittuq will require considerable advance planning and preparation, and we have tried to help in this process by providing basic information as well as citing sources for further details. We hope that you will be able to visit Auyuittuq. If you are seeking a different kind of experience you will surely find it in "the land that never melts".

Roger Wilson,

Assistant Chief, Interpretation,
Quebec Region, Parks Canada

Acknowledgements

As co-ordinator/editor of this book I have had the pleasure of working with many people. Although space requirements prevent my thanking everyone here by name, no one has been forgotten.

Special thanks are due Gifford Miller, Raymond Bradley, Peter Schledermann and Patrick Baird, the authors of the various chapters. Your suggestion that Parks Canada produce a book of this kind was most timely and your subsequent enthusiasm and co-operation were invaluable.

David MacAdam's contribution of many of the wildflower photographs made a difficult search much easier.

I am deeply grateful to Jean-Luc Grondin for his magnificent paintings of the birds. They are not only important aids to identification, they are also fine works of art.

Last, but not least, I wish to thank my many co-workers. Your help and enthusiasm are greatly appreciated.

Since becoming Minister of Indian and Northern Affairs, I have had great pleasure in seeing the steadily mounting interest in Auyuittuq National Park on Baffin Island. The park has attracted visitors from all over the world and has provided them with the challenges and satisfactions that only the arctic environment can generate.

As with all of our National Parks, Auyuittuq represents a natural region of national significance. It is also one of our most remote parks and as a result is not likely to be visited by the majority of Canadians. This book is an effort to make Auyuittuq more "accessible". It is part of a continuing effort to bring to Canadians the riches represented in their National Parks.

I hope that in reading it you will discover for yourself the fragile beauty that makes Auyuittuq National Park one of Canada's treasures.

Judd Buchanan,
Minister of Indian and Northern Affairs

The Land That Never Melts

1. The Shaping of a Land: Geology, Climate and Ice Age History

Gifford H. Miller
Raymond S. Bradley

Dedicated to the Inuit people, who probably know better the subtleties of their land than all the scientists who will study it.

The Geology and Physical Evolution of Cumberland Peninsula

The first view most visitors will have of the park is from the air. As one flies across Cumberland Sound in summer, after leaving the subdued landscape of Hall Peninsula, the Penny Highlands appear on the horizon as a white-tipped mass of rock and snow. As they come closer to view, individual glaciers and ice caps become discernible among the ruggedly dissected mountains and fiords that dominate Cumberland Peninsula. Presiding over this landscape is the Penny Ice Cap, a vast expanse of ice and snow mantling 6,000 square kilometres of the peninsula and drained by outlet glaciers on all sides, some up to twenty-five kilometres long and extending gradually to the sea, others dropping dramatically from heights of 1,500 metres to nearly sea level in only a few kilometres. That first look at Auyuittuq National Park is unforgettable, a portrait of slow-moving, but powerful rivers of ice which have, over seemingly endless time, sculptured this panorama out of the hard rock of the peninsula.

Indeed, it is the rock and snow that at first overwhelm the other aspects of the park. The over-abundance of rock in the Arctic prompted a highly placed government official to claim, after an uncomfortable journey in the north long ago, that the Lord made the earth and all the living things on it in five days; on the sixth day he made the Northwest Territories, and on the seventh day he sat back and threw rocks at it. While the story probably has little factual

1

basis, visitors to Auyuittuq National Park will undoubtedly be first impressed by the rocks—from the towering sheer faces of Mounts Asgard, Thor, Overlord and others to the unending rock-strewn hill-slopes left by the receding ice-age glaciers.

The bedrock core of the peninsula belongs to the vast geological province known as the Canadian Shield, and rocks in the park are similar to those of much of northeastern Canada and adjacent west Greenland. The Canadian Shield province in fact underlies nearly five million square kilometres of central and eastern Canada, extending down into the United States, and may represent the earliest beginnings of the North American continent. Most of the shield rocks on Cumberland Peninsula were deposited originally as sedimentary and volcanic rocks approximately two to three billion years ago, at a time when the climate and configuration of the continents were vastly different than they are today. The changing configuration of the continental land masses is known as *continental drift*. Geologists now believe that the continents may move about on the denser underlying crust at the rate of a few centimetres per year. At a late period in the formation of some of the rocks in the park, in fact, Cumberland Peninsula occupied a position not far from the present equator. After the original rocks were

Geologic Time		Beginning of each time interval in years BP
Era	*Period*	
Cenozoic	Quaternary	2—3 million
	Tertiary	65 million
Mesozoic	Cretaceous	130 million
	Jurassic	185 million
	Triassic	220 million
	Paleozoic	550 million
Pre-Cambrian		4 or more billion

deposited, they underwent extensive metamorphism. Then, early in the Paleozoic era, when life-forms were first spreading over the earth, the eastern Arctic was inundated by an extensive shallow sea and the shield rocks were covered by a thick blanket of marine sediments, rich in fossils of marine life. The shallow seas probably advanced and receded across the region several times, but in the late Paleozoic, some two to three hundred million years agó, the land was uplifted, and Cumberland Peninsula has probably remained above sea level ever since.

The continents were nearing their present positions by the end of the Mesozoic era. At that time Greenland and Baffin Island were joined, or separated only by a narrow, shallow sea. The prevailing climate was temperate, and lush vegetation and large trees grew on what is now Cumberland Peninsula. About sixty million years ago, Greenland and Baffin Island began to split apart. In the early stages this was accompanied by extensive volcanic activity at the margins of the two land masses. The resultant lava flows are preserved on Baffin Island on the northern shore of Cumberland Peninsula, and similar lavas formed at the same time have been found on western Greenland, directly across Davis Strait. Cape Searle (Figure 1), adjacent to the park, is composed primarily of lava which formed at this time.

The separation of these two land masses was accompanied by uplift of not only eastern Baffin Island but of the entire eastern margin of Canada as well. The increased relief along the eastern margin intensified erosion until eventually all of the relatively soft marine sediments that had been laid down on the shield rocks were eroded from the peninsula. On western Baffin Island and in Foxe Basin where the relief is gentler and erosion has been less extensive, large portions of the old marine sediments are preserved. However, on Cumberland Peninsula today, except for the few narrow outcrops of volcanic and sedimentary rocks between Cape Searle and Cape Dyer, the bedrock is composed exclusively of the crystalline rocks of the Canadian Shield.

The erosion of the sedimentary rock cover exposed the old landscape of the shield rocks, which had formed long before the inundation by the sea. River valleys, originally formed several hundred million years ago, may again have been occupied by streams. It seems likely that the landscape of Baffin Island, prior to the onset of the ice ace, was a broad, rolling countryside, with well-established river valleys separated by rolling mountains. These pre-existing river valleys, themselves probably oriented along lines of weakness in the bedrock, were also responsible for much of the orientation of the present fiord and valley systems, for the advancing glaciers were thickest and most vigorous in the valleys. With the coming of the ice age, the climate of the Arctic deteriorated, and its appearance was dramatically and forever altered.

Glaciers and Climate

Although the Canadian landscape has its origin rooted deep in the geological past, the single most significant event in the creation of its appearance today was the coming of the great ice sheets. The

Fig. 1. Cape Searle, a small but prominent island overlooking Davis Strait, has special geologic and biologic features. The horizontally-banded cliffs are composed of lava formed by volcanic eruptions when Greenland and Baffin Island began to split apart some sixty million years ago. Beneath the lava are coal-bearing sedimentary rocks—testament to a time when a milder climate reigned over Cumberland Peninsula. Along the inaccessible lava face of Cape Searle nests one of the world's largest fulmar colonies. This photo, looking southeast toward Cape Dyer, was taken in late August during the particularly severe summer of 1972 when sea ice persisted along northern Cumberland Peninsula throughout the summer.

build-up and decay of ice sheets covering vast tracts of North America and Europe occurred during the *Quaternary* (more or less synonymous with *Pleistocene*) Period, approximately the last two million years of the earth's history. This short period, while barely perceptible within the broader framework of geologic time, so greatly altered our planet's physical and biological appearance that the pre-Quaternary landscape would probably be completely foreign to us today. The erosion, deposition and melt waters of the Quaternary ice sheets changed the face of the earth it passed over, and the associated climatic shifts influenced widespread biological change, including the emergence of man. It is the period of the earth's history we best understand, yet the causes of the dramatic climatic shifts still remain obscure. Similarly, although the mountains and overall form of Baffin Island resulted from continental movements and associated crustal uplift occurring several tens of millions of years ago, the modification of Cumberland Peninsula into the spectacular landscape of today is dominantly a product of Quaternary events.

The onset of the Quaternary Period is recorded throughout the world as a lowering of air and ocean temperatures, and although there is evidence that the Antarctic Ice Sheet existed as early as forty million years ago, the cyclical growth and decay of the vast continental ice sheets of North America and Europe are Quaternary phenomena. At present, 10 per cent of the earth is covered by glacial ice, of which fully 95 per cent lies within the relatively stable Antarctic and Greenland ice sheets. During the Quaternary glaciations, up to 30 per cent of the earth was ice-covered. The growth of the North American, and to a lesser extent the European, ice sheets was largely responsible for this increase.

At the height of the last glaciation, the North American continent lay beneath three major and several lesser ice sheets. Dominating them all was the *Laurentide Ice Sheet*, the largest of the northern hemisphere ice sheets, covering nearly all of Canada east of the Rocky Mountains. An independent ice sheet complex, the *Cordilleran Ice Sheet*, covered much of the Canadian Rockies and extended to the Pacific Ocean, while the high arctic islands lay beneath another independent ice sheet complex. (The outlines of these great ice sheets are shown in Figure 3). The Laurentide Ice Sheet is the only one of these which noticeably affected Baffin Island, and this chapter will concentrate on its history.

Although the Laurentide Ice Sheet grew and disintegrated many times throughout the Quaternary, it has left little direct evidence of

Fig. 2. An unnamed glacier in Nedlukseak Fiord which, as recently as 100 years ago, reached the sea. The medial moraines indicate that this glacier is fed from several independent sources.

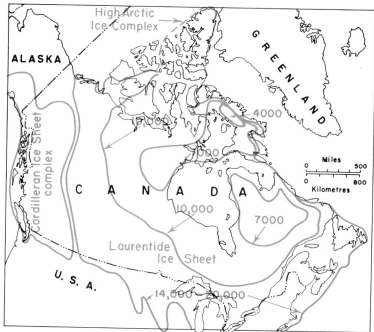

Fig. 3. The margins of the Laurentide Ice Sheet and the Cordilleran and high arctic ice sheet complexes at the last glacial maximum. The outline of the Laurentide Ice Sheet at various times during its wastage are also indicated, showing the general pattern of ice-recession toward the northeast. The nature of the contact between Laurentide and high arctic ice is not, as yet, well known.

the earliest expansions as younger advances destroyed most of the older deposits. However, evidence from the deep sea floor and from terrestrial deposits related to a glaciation but which formed outside the perimeter of the ice sheets, suggests the major glaciations were separated from one another by *interglacials*—periods of relative warmth and minimal land ice, similar to the climate of the interglacial we live in at present. Within each glaciation, major fluctuations of the ice margins define *stades*, periods of extensive ice coverage, and *interstades*, periods of minimal ice coverage. Only within the most recent glaciation, the *Wisconsin Glaciation*, is the timing of the stades and interstades known; best known is the *Late Wisconsin Stade*, the most recent advance of the Laurentide

Ice Sheet which occurred between about 25,000 and 7,000 years ago. The glacial-interglacial cycles appear to be more or less regularly spaced with a duration of 100,000 to 150,000 years, the majority of which is the glacial portion of the cycle, with each interglaciation lasting only 10,000 to 15,000 years. Fossil plants, found in deposits of the last interglacial in central and eastern Baffin Island, indicate that the climate then was slightly warmer than that of the present interglacial.

Growth and Decay of the Laurentide Ice Sheet

The development of an ice sheet of continental proportions in northern Canada requires an extended period of abundant snowfall and reduced summer melting over much of the area. A climatic deterioration of this sort does not affect all portions of northern Canada equally, for some areas are more sensitive to changes in climate than are others. Probably the area most sensitive to increased snowfall or decreased snowmelt is the plateau region of central Baffin Island, and it is over this region that the last glaciation originated, and presumably the next will originate as well.

Shortly after central Baffin Island became snow-covered, similar events probably occurred over the Keewatin and Labrador uplands to the west and east of Hudson Bay, producing a vast thin snowfield over much of northern Canada. As the snowfields continued to accumulate snow and thicken, under the influence of gravity they eventually began to flow to lower regions, filling Hudson Bay and ultimately merging into a single ice sheet covering northern Canada. Before it could flow southward, the ice sheet had to thicken appreciably. As it thickened, requiring continued heavy snowfall derived from moisture in the air masses passing over the ice sheet, it attained a considerable height, and resembled the topographic barrier of a mountain range. Thus, in the same way that moisture from the Pacific Ocean results in heavy rainfall on the western side of the mountains of the Pacific Northwest while the eastern side remains comparatively dry in a *precipitation shadow*, precipitation on the Laurentide Ice Sheet, which was primarily derived from the oceans at middle latitudes, was probably greatest on the southern portion and least on the northern portions. Unlike mountains, however, an ice sheet moves, and in response to the heavier snowfall on its southern regions the centre of the ice sheet can be expected to migrate southward, toward its source of nourishment. Consequently, the northern regions would receive increasingly less snowfall (precipitation shadow effect), and because they would experience less frequent incursions of relatively warm, moist southerly air, the area would become a *polar desert* (cold and dry). Thus, in the geologic record one might expect the arctic ice to have been most extensive during the early phases of a glaciation when the centre of the ice sheet was in the north, and to become progressively reduced as the centre migrated southward depriving the northern regions of precipitation. On the other hand, the reverse activity along the southern margin should have resulted in the most extensive ice formation occurring toward the latter portion of a glaciation. The geologic evidence supports this supposition.

The timing of these events can only be roughly estimated. The development of a more or less continuous thin snowfield over northern Canada could be accomplished in a few hundred years, but the time involved for such a snowfield to develop into a continental ice sheet impinging on southern Canada would be considerably longer. Estimates vary, but even with substantial increases in winter snowfall and reduced melting, it would require 10,000 to 15,000 years.

At its maximum extent in the Late Wisconsin Stade, the Laurentide Ice Sheet covered nearly all of central Canada and the Maritime provinces, and extended into midwestern and northeastern United States. In the west, it had expanded into the Prairie provinces to the base of the Rocky Mountains, which at that time lay beneath the independent Cordilleran Ice Sheet complex. At this time, the Laurentide Ice Sheet covered nearly thirteen million square kilometres, roughly the size of the present Antarctic Ice Sheet and nearly six times larger than the Greenland Ice Sheet. While the ice sheet was most extensive, present day Hudson Bay, located near the centre of the former ice sheet, lay beneath 3,000 to 4,000 metres (10,000 to 13,000 feet) of ice!

The break-up and final disappearance of the Laurentide Ice Sheet at the close of the Wisconsin Glaciation has been studied and mapped in detail, although the cause of its disintegration is still unclear. The timing of the deglacial phases is documented by means of radiocarbon (^{14}C) dating techniques.* Along most of its southern and western margins the ice sheet remained at or near its maximum

*Ages determined by the radiocarbon method are given technically as radiocarbon years BP (before present), with present understood to be 1950 A.D. Radiocarbon years may differ slightly from actual calendar years, but this difference is not appreciable. Radiocarbon dating is capable of determining the age of organic samples as old as 70,000 years, but is, in general, restricted to the last 25,000 to 30,000 years. Most dates cited as less than 30,000 years are based on radiocarbon analyses.

Fig. 4. The entrance to Pangnirtung Pass from Pangnirtung Fiord, showing the characteristic U-shaped profile of a glaciated valley.

extent until 15,000 years ago, after which it began to recede rapidly, although short-lived readvances did occur. The northwestern and northeastern margins did not begin to recede until somewhat later, and on eastern Baffin Island, the Laurentide Ice Sheet remained at its maximum extent until shortly before 8,000 years ago. As the ice sheet melted, the final vestiges were located on the plateaus of Keewatin, Labrador and Baffin Island, the same areas where it is thought to have originated. The residual ice caps disappeared from Keewatin and Labrador by 5,000 years ago, but the Baffin Island residual ice sheet receded more slowly, and the Barnes Ice Cap situated on the plateau of north central Baffin Island, and possibly the northwestern portion of the Penny Ice Cap, are thought to be true remnants of the Laurentide Ice Sheet.

Modification of the Landscape by Glaciers

The inundation of an area by actively eroding ice dramatically modifies the former landscape, and it is probably for their unique erosional and depositional abilities that glaciers are best known. Cumberland Peninsula has been glaciated by both the Laurentide Ice Sheet (continental ice) and local alpine or *cirque glaciers*, each producing somewhat different characteristic landforms. It is doubtful that the peninsula has ever been completely inundated by continental ice, as even during the most extensive recorded glaciations, the mountain and valley systems channelled the flow of continental ice into large *outlet glaciers,* restricted to the fiords and interior valleys. These outlet glaciers were active erosive agents which, following old river valleys and lines of weakness in the local bedrock, over-deepened and straightened the shallow valleys until, after numerous successive glaciations, they formed the deep fiord and valley systems of today. These U-shaped glacial troughs were probably established early in the Quaternary, and because they effectively diverted continental outlet glaciers to the ocean, most of the higher mountains were subsequently protected from modification by continental ice. Within the park, the only large area to have been extensively glaciated by the Laurentide Ice Sheet is the plateau area around the western margin of the Penny Ice Cap.

The mountains of the peninsula, while escaping modification by continental glaciers, were ideally situated for the development of local alpine glaciers. During the major glaciations, small glaciers which developed on the high land not covered by continental ice eroded back into the mountain masses to eventually form *cirques,* bowl-like hollows high in the mountains. Many of the cirques in the park are still occupied by glaciers, but others are presently ice-free and glaciers will only reform in them under the effects of a climate more severe than the present one. As alpine glaciers eroded their cirques more deeply into the mountains, the surrounding ridges became increasingly sharpened. In some areas several cirques have been eroded into the same mountain forming *arêtes, horns* and *serrated ridges.* The degree of development of these alpine forms is an indication of the length of time cirque glaciers have been active. The superbly developed alpine glacial forms between Pangnirtung and Kingnait passes reflect several hundred thousand years of continued alpine glacial erosion, and indicate that continental ice, which would have effectively smoothed the jagged peaks, probably did not cover the area during that time.

It is the combination of large outlet glaciers from the Laurentide Ice Sheet and small local cirque glaciers that has created the contrasts that make the Auyuittuq National Park scenery so breathtaking. As the Laurentide Ice Sheet advanced onto the peninsula from the west, it was channelled by Pangnirtung Pass into Cumberland Sound in the south and Davis Strait in the north, and in the process eroded the pass into a spectacularly deep U-shaped valley, overshadowed by the austere peaks of the Penny Highlands.

Fig. 5. The effect of glacial erosion on a previously unglaciated
river valley. The valley is straightened, and its profile altered from
V-shaped to a U-shaped form.

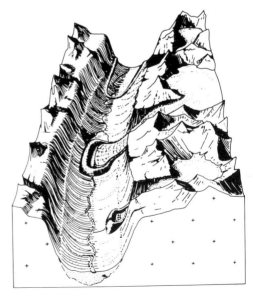

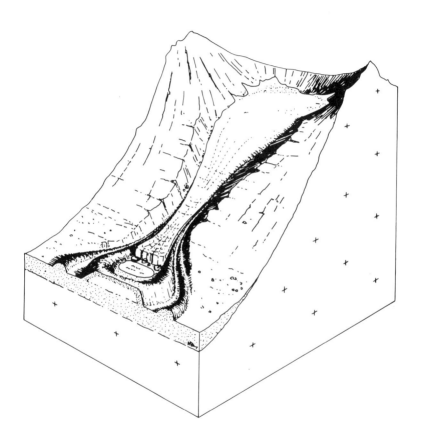

Fig. 6. A model of a typical cirque glacier of the major valleys on Cumberland Peninsula. The massive appearance of the fresh moraines fronting these glaciers is misleading, as the core of these moraines is composed of remnant glacial ice, and comprises more than 90 per cent of their volume.

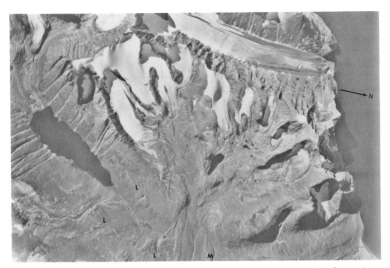

Fig. 7. Vertical aerial photograph of a late Wisconsin terminal moraine formed by a cirque glacier complex between Narpaing Fiord and Okoa Bay near the northern edge of the park. At the last glacial maximum, the individual cirque glaciers expanded and merged into a single large glacier that formed the moraine (M) at the bottom centre of the photograph. Remnant lateral moraines (L) were formed during an earlier, more extensive glaciation. The snouts of the present cirque glaciers are fronted by recently-formed terminal moraines.

During the most extensive glaciations, Pangnirtung Pass could not handle the incoming volume of ice, which consequently overflowed to the east into Kingnait Pass via the Naksakjua and June River valleys. While the continental glaciers were scouring the passes, local cirque glaciers were sculpturing the highlands into a rugged alpine topography of cirques, knife-like ridges and pinnacled peaks. The massive, large-scale modifications of continental ice, complemented by the detailed sculpturing of the mountains by alpine glaciers, has produced some of the most primitive, and strikingly rugged landscapes anywhere.

The glaciers not only left their mark in the form of eroded valley and fiord systems and alpine highlands, but also in less conspicuous depositional features such as *moraines,* composed of shattered rock debris transported by the moving ice to the margins of the glacier. *Lateral* and *terminal moraines* show us the outlines of the former glaciers. Moraines formed during the Wisconsin Glaciation are subdued and less obvious than moraines of modern glaciers, but can be seen by observant visitors throughout the park along the less-steep portions of the fiord and valley walls. Visitors will notice several sets of lateral moraines 400 to 500 metres (about 1,500 feet) above sea level on both sides of Pangnirtung Fiord as they fly into the park from the south. Well-developed moraines encircle Mount Duval above the hamlet of Pangnirtung, and may be seen at about 600 metres (2,000 feet) above the sea along North Pangnirtung Fiord on the flight to Broughton Island. Because they are subdued, the older moraines are less conspicuous from the ground.

At a smaller scale, many other clues may be found of glacial episodes. As glaciers flow through a region they pick up all the loose rock debris, concentrating most of it in the lower layers of the ice. When this debris-laden ice passes over particularly resistant bedrock it may polish or scour the underlying rock. Large sections of polished bedrock slabs may be found within the park: some are in Pangnirtung Pass, but the best exposures are in the main Nedluk-

Fig. 8. Evidence of a glacier's passage may be found as striated bedrock. This particular example is the result of two distinct glaciations: the striations coming toward the viewer were etched by a fiord glacier advance; later a side valley glacier advanced obliquely over the locality producing the grooves which run from upper left to lower right in the picture.

seak valley, and west of the Penny Ice Cap. These polished slabs usually contain *striations*—grooves and scratches made by rock fragments as they are dragged over the bedrock under pressure from the weight of overlying ice. Striations indicate the direction of ice movement. In some localities, striations made by glaciers flowing from different directions at different times are preserved on the same slab, as in Figure 8.

During the waning phases of a glaciation the glaciers are often sluggish and large portions may become stagnant, ceasing to flow. As the ice melts, rocks, which had been incorporated into the glacier, slowly settle out and are deposited on the ground surface. Because the rocks settle more or less randomly, they are often deposited in precarious positions. The larger rocks may end up perched above the surrounding bedrock on smaller rock fragments. Rocks which are everywhere separated from the underlying rock by only a few small rocks are called *perched boulders* and are common throughout the glaciated regions of the park, although few are more spectacular than the one in Figure 9.

Fig. 9. This massive boulder, weighing several tons, lies perched above the bedrock on three small rock fragments. Such perched boulders, left by the receding ice-age glaciers, are used as evidence for the extent of glaciation. This one is in June River Valley between Pangnirtung and Kingnait Passes.

Glaciers and Relative Sea Level

> "On one occasion, when I was speaking with Tookoolito concerning her people, she said, 'Innuits all think this earth once covered with water.' I asked her why they thought so. She answered, 'Did you ever see little stones, like clams and such things as live in the sea, away up on the mountains?' "
>
> (C.F. Hall, *Life with the Esquimaux*, 1865)

The mountain scenery, striking though it is, is only one product of a glaciation. The growth of a continental ice sheet requires the storage on the continents of a considerable amount of water in the form of ice and snow. This gain of water on the continents is directly reflected by a reduction of water in the world's oceans. There is now good evidence that during the maximum of the late Wisconsin glacial stade, world sea level was 100 metres (330 feet) lower than present. The volume of water which must be removed from the oceans to lower sea level by 100 metres is roughly equivalent to the volume locked up as ice in the major continental ice sheets of that time. With world sea level dropped by 100 metres, all the ocean floor covered at present by less than 100 metres of water was dry land. Thus, where Alaska and Siberia are now separated by a shallow sea, during full glacial episodes they were connected by a stretch of dry land called the Bering Land Bridge, or *Beringia*. This bridge between the North American and Asian continents afforded an easy migration route to the Americas, and was probably the path by which earliest man arrived in the Western world.

The volume of the Laurentide Ice Sheet (about thirty million cubic kilometres or a weight of roughly two trillion tons for those who like figures) represents a considerable increase in weight on the North American continent. How is the addition of this weight going to affect the continents? According to our best understanding of the earth's crust, the continental land masses are "floating" on underlying semi-molten mantle rock. The depth to which the continents sink into the mantle is directly proportional to the weight of the overlying land mass (*isostasy*). Thus, under mountainous regions the continent sinks deeper into the mantle than under lowland areas. Like the formation of new mountains, the build-up of continental ice sheets several thousand metres in thickness causes the continental crust to sink under the weight of the additional load. Ice (which geologist consider as rock) is only about one-third as dense as ordinary rock, hence the amount of crustal subsidence (*glacio-isostasy*) is equivalent to one-third the thickness of the over-lying ice. Thus, at the centre of a 1,000-metre thick ice sheet, the crust would be depressed by slightly over 300 metres, and by decreasing amounts away from the center. Because the crust is rather rigid, the depression of land extends for some distance beyond the ice margin. Although the adjustment of the land to an ice load is rather slow and takes several thousand years to reach equilibrium, by the end of the Late Wisconsin Stade the land depression was nearly in equilibrium with the ice load.

During the break-up of the Laurentide Ice Sheet, the ice load was removed more rapidly than the sluggish mantle rock could respond, and as a result much of the land that became ice-free was still rising, returning to the position it had before the glacial loading. On the shores of Cumberland Peninsula, beaches which formed soon after the ice disappeared were uplifted as the land rose to its preglacial elevation. The situation is, however, further complicated, for as the continental ice sheets melted, returning their

Fig. 10. An old beach several metres above sea level exposed by wave action at the northern tip of Broughton Island. Beach deposits, which extend up the hill-slope to forty-five metres above the sea, formed here more than 35,000 years ago. The settlement of Broughton Island is built on an extension of the same beach.

stored water to the ocean, sea level rose. Although both the land surface and sea level were rising as the ice sheet wasted, over most of Cumberland Peninsula the isostatic uplift of the earth's crust exceeded the sea level rise, and beaches originally formed at sea level may be found several tens of metres above present sea level. In general the highest of these beaches are between twenty and seventy metres above the sea, although in at least one locality near Kivitoo, beach deposits from a very old glaciation have been found more than 200 metres above sea level. Lower beaches may be seen at the heads of most fiords, and may be preserved in protected valley mouths along the fiords. The hamlets of Pangnirtung and Broughton Island are both built at least in part on old beaches, and the roads are often littered with the fragments of sea shells that lived on these deposits when they were being formed. The ages of these beaches varies considerably; most shells from Broughton Island are more than 35,000 years old, whereas the highest beaches (fifty metres) at Pangnirtung are between 8,000 and 9,000 years old. Lower beaches are generally younger.

Glaciation of Cumberland Peninsula

Because of its high mountains, deep fiord and valley systems, and location on the margin of the former Laurentide Ice Sheet, Cumberland Peninsula has a complex and varied history of glaciation. Deposits formed by advances of local cirque glaciers are juxtaposed with those formed by Laurentide outlet glaciers, and deposits of several ages related to both types of glacial activity are represented in the area. The occurrence in the northern portion of the park of glacial deposits older than the Wisconsin Glaciation provides some of the oldest known direct evidence for fluctuations of the northeastern margin of the Laurentide Ice Sheet. The relative sea level oscillations associated with the growth and decay of the continental ice sheets and with the crustal depression caused by the glacial loading of the continent, have noticeably affected the area. The relationships between the resultant *raised marine deposits* (deposits formed at sea level and subsequently elevated above their original position by glacio-isostatic uplift) and glacial features provide many of the clues with which we interpret the glacial history of the peninsula. *Submerged marine deposits* have been located on submarine profiles, but are restricted to the outer fringes of the peninsula where the sea level rise exceeded the glacio-isostatic uplift of the land.

Earliest Glaciations

Evidence of extensive glaciations predating the Wisconsin Glaciation is found as *glacial till* (unsorted rock debris deposited directly by the ice) above and beyond the limits of the most extensive Wisconsin advance. The old till is distinguished from Wisconsin till on the basis of *rock weathering*, the slow process of rock disintegration caused by normal environmental factors. Moraines originally consist of fresh rock fragments which in time become rounded and pitted, the less resistant portions disintegrating most rapidly. The relief of resistant veins (principally quartz veins) in the rock is most indicative of these weathering differences. Quartz vein relief on Wisconsin till is generally less than two millimetres (barely perceptible), whereas on pre-Wisconsin deposits it is commonly two to five centimetres (one to two inches). The rate of rock weathering in the Arctic is considerably slower than at lower latitudes, and major

Fig. 11. The surface of a rock which has probably been exposed to weathering processes for several hundred thousand years. The quartz vein, because of its resistance to weathering, stands several centimetres above the less-resistant surrounding rock. In other areas the rocks are noticeably less weathered, suggesting these areas have been glaciated more recently than the highly weathered rock areas.

differences in weathering of similar rock types must reflect a long time interval. The extensive weathering of pre-Wisconsin till relative to adjacent Wisconsin till suggests the former is considerably older. Weathering differences are not readily detectable between deposits of the various Wisconsin stades.

The most accessible major pre-Wisconsin deposits are in the extensive coastal lowlands between the mouths of Narpaing and Quajon Fiords on the northern edge of the park. Here a large expanse of glacial till and *outwash*, sediment deposited by meltwater from the fiord glaciers, lies interbedded with raised marine deposits (Figure 12). Low cliffs, formed by wave erosion into these headlands, reveal at least three units of glacial origin, each separated by marine sediments containing shells of fossil molluscs and microscopic organisms. Although even the youngest of these is beyond the range of radiocarbon dating methods, an approximate age has been obtained through an alternate dating technique utilizing the decay of trace amounts of Uranium. These analyses indicate that shells in the youngest (uppermost) marine sediments, which are overlain by a moraine formed during the earliest Wisconsin stade, lived sometime between 100,000 and 150,000 years ago. Glacial and marine deposits which lie beneath this unit must have been deposited even earlier and may be of considerable antiquity, although as yet no absolute ages are available.

The Last Glaciation

Deposits formed during the Wisconsin Glaciation are the most common in the park and enable us to reconstruct glacial events during that period with reasonable accuracy. Recent studies suggest that the maximum Wisconsin ice coverage of the peninsula occurred early during the last glaciation, and that even then large areas of the northeastern and southeastern portions of the peninsula were not covered by actively eroding ice. During succeeding stades of the Wisconsin Glaciation ice coverage decreased, and during the Late Wisconsin Stade ice coverage was least extensive. The progressive diminution of ice cover throughout the Wisconsin is a direct consequence of the southerly migration of the Laurentide Ice Sheet centre as discussed previously. During the initial build-up of the ice sheet its central and thickest portion was in the north, and winter snowfall must have been correspondingly high to nourish the growing ice sheet. At this time the northern regions experienced their most extensive glaciations. As the ice sheet dome thickened and migrated southward, the driving force for ice movement (ice

Fig. 12. The development of the extensive lowlands between Quajon and Narpaing Fiords.

a. The original land surface and sea level.

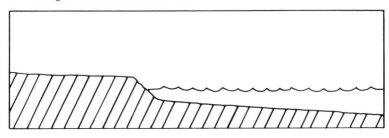

b. The land surface is depressed by the build-up of the North American ice sheet. Before the glacier reaches the locality, marine sediments may be laid down, including the shells of marine animals.

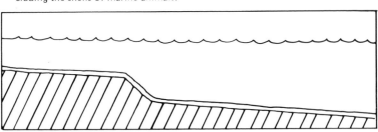

c. The glacier arrives and deposits outwash and till over the locality. Some of the underlying sediments may be disturbed or eroded by the advancing ice.

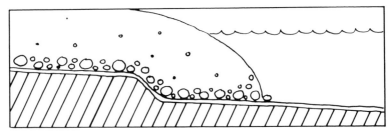

d. The glacier recedes and the land begins to rise to its original position as the ice sheet melts and removes its load from the continent. Until the land emerges from the sea, marine sediments may be deposited.

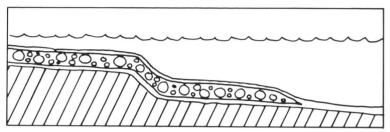

e. Land and sea level return to their original positions.

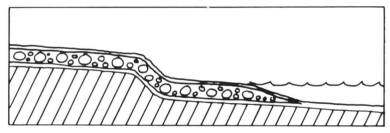

f. The sediments record the effects of three glacial cycles (a. to e. above). The bottom sediments are the oldest, and fossil shells in the marine sediments may provide clues as to the ages of the glaciations.

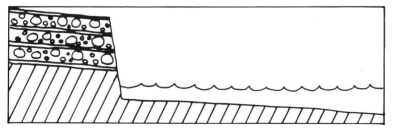

thickness) and winter snowfall decreased across the arctic regions; consequently the intensity of glaciation was diminished.

Although the detailed outline of early Wisconsin ice limits is not precisely known, the general pattern is understood. At this time, the incoming volume of Laurentide ice in Pangnirtung Pass was more than could be diverted by the pass and adjoining fiords, and the Naksakjua and June River Valleys carried the excess ice to the sea via Kingnait Pass. However, the amount of ice that passed through these valleys at this time must have been relatively small, as pre-Wisconsin till occurs less than 200 metres above the passes opening into these valleys from Pangnirtung Pass. The outlet glacier diverted down Pangnirtung Fiord covered the area of the hamlet of Pangnirtung with more than 500 metres of ice. On the northern edge of the park, Broughton Island Settlement lay under 600 metres of ice and the major fiords to the north all carried extensive outlet glaciers several hundred metres thick that ended in terminal lobes at the fiord mouths. What is now the Penny Ice Cap was overwhelmed by Laurentide ice, and *erratic* limestone rocks in early Wisconsin till suggest that material was brought to the area from limestone outcrops in Foxe Basin and on western Baffin Island 200 to 300 kilometres west of the peninsula.

A shift to milder climatic conditions caused the withdrawal of early Wisconsin ice. Ocean temperatures increased and may even have been warmer than they are now. The Icelandic scallop, a shell species found at present only in warmer water south of Cumberland Peninsula, has been found in raised marine deposits formed during this time in Quajon Fiord and on eastern Broughton Island. This relatively warm interstade separated the early Wisconsin from subsequent Wisconsin advances, and a Uranium series date on the associated mollusc shells suggests it occurred around 60,000 years ago.

Following the interstadial, Laurentide ice again advanced onto the peninsula, in some places nearly as extensively as during the early Wisconsin advance. This period, generally referred to as the Mid Wisconsin Stade, is complex and as yet incompletely understood, and in some areas may involve a second, very restricted advance. The Pangnirtung area was again covered by a thick outlet glacier, although ice only just reached the present settlement of Broughton Island. Shells 40,000 to 50,000 years old which were ploughed up by the ice crossing the straits separating Broughton from mainland Baffin Island may be found in till immediately above the Hudson's Bay Company store on Broughton Island. During the smaller of the Mid Wisconsin advances, neither Broughton Island nor Pangnirtung were ice-covered.

Most visitors (scientists and non-scientists alike), seeing the degree of present glaciation, quite naturally suppose that during the last glacial maximum, when ice had advanced over Canada and into the United States, the area must surely have been buried under a vast ice sheet. Surprisingly, it wasn't. Indeed, one of the most remarkable facts about this area is that at the last glacial maximum some local cirque glaciers and outlet glaciers of local mountain ice caps were actually smaller than they are today! Climatic reconstructions based on the response of different glaciers suggest that the park area was a frozen desert during the late Wisconsin; summer temperatures averaged four degrees Celsius colder than at present and winter snowfall was only one-quarter of current amounts.

This particularly cold and arid stade lasted from about 25,000 to 9,000 years ago. Throughout the stade, the influence of Laurentide ice on the peninsula was minimal. Outlet glaciers only just reached Pangnirtung Pass, and even then portions of the pass floor remained ice-free, while Kingnait Pass was probably completely devoid of ice. Neither Pangnirtung nor Broughton Island settlements were ice-covered, and in the northern regions Laurentide ice was restricted to the proximity of the heads of most fiords. In the large ice-free areas at this time, local glaciers were free to respond independently to the Wisconsin climate. Some glaciers advanced up to fourteen kilometres beyond their present termini, whereas others remained more or less stationary.

All shells found in raised marine deposits related to the maximum stand of both Laurentide and local glacier advances on the peninsula have radiocarbon ages of 8,000 to 8,500 years BP. Shells from similar deposits elsewhere on Baffin Island are all of approximately the same age, suggesting that the glacial history of the peninsula is similar to that of the rest of eastern Baffin Island. Sometime between 8,500 and 8,000 years ago the marine environment improved abruptly, and a variety of relatively warm-water shell species migrated into the region. At about the same time precipitation and temperatures on the land increased. For a short while the precipitation increases actually made the glaciers expand slightly, but soon the rise in temperature became dominant and by 8,000 years ago glaciers were receding throughout the region. By 7,000 years ago most fiord heads were ice-free and local glaciers had receded behind their present margins, and by 5,500 years ago the distribution of glacial ice was less extensive than at present.

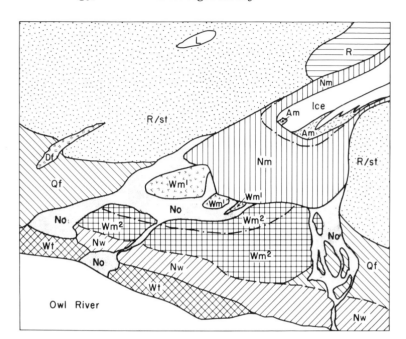

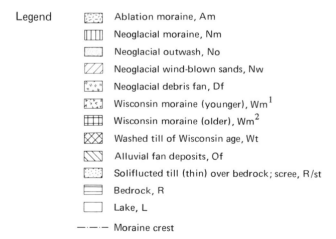

Legend

- Ablation moraine, Am
- Neoglacial moraine, Nm
- Neoglacial outwash, No
- Neoglacial wind-blown sands, Nw
- Neoglacial debris fan, Df
- Wisconsin moraine (younger), Wm^1
- Wisconsin moraine (older), Wm^2
- Washed till of Wisconsin age, Wt
- Alluvial fan deposits, Of
- Soliflucted till (thin) over bedrock; scree, R/st
- Bedrock, R
- Lake, L
- —·—·— Moraine crest

Fig. 13. A glacier in northern Pangnirtung Pass, and a geologic map of the associated superficial deposits. The Wisconsin-aged moraines lying immediately in front of the modern moraine indicate that this glacier is nearly as extensive at present as it was at the last glacial maximum.

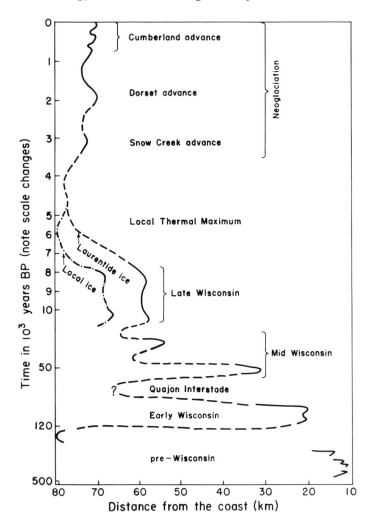

Fig. 14. A schematic representation of the past glaciations of the Cumberland Peninsula area. Note that the time-scale changes, and that we know more about more recent events than we do of the earliest glaciations.

Recent Glacier Fluctuations and Lichenometry

The disappearance of the Laurentide Ice Sheet and the shrinkage of most local and outlet glaciers at the end of the Wisconsin Glaciation were caused by a general shift in the world climate to the relatively warmer conditions of the present interglacial. Maximum temperatures were probably warmer than those of the present, while sea ice and glaciers were less extensive. During the latter phases of this warmest period of our present interglacial the first people, following the ice-free passageways and relatively abundant game, migrated into the eastern Canadian Arctic. However, after several millenia of relatively warm conditions the climate began to deteriorate, and in response to climatic oscillations between relatively "glacial" and "non-glacial" modes, glaciers began a series of small advances and recessions. This period of renewed glacier growth which began about 3,500 years ago has been called *Neoglaciation*, and glacier variations are recorded throughout the park as suites of *Neoglacial* moraines. These moraines generally reflect minor adjustments of glacier termini to the small-scale climatic fluctuations. Because of the regional scarcity of organic matter it is not possible to date these moraines by conventional radiocarbon techniques. However, a novel method has been employed utilizing the abundant lichens which grow on these fresh rock surfaces.

Lichens are actually composed of two plants: green algal cells interspersed in strands of fungus which coexist in a *symbiotic relationship*, each benefiting from the presence of the other. They are among the most adaptable of living organisms and are found in the most extreme environments of heat, aridity and cold. Lichens are abundant throughout the Arctic, and at higher elevations or in rocky areas without soil they are the dominant vegetation. Certain *crustose* or *rock lichens*—very thin lichens fastened everywhere to the rock surface—grow very slowly in a generally circular pattern. It has been noted that these lichens are among the first plant colonizers on fresh moraines and that certain lichen species are larger and more abundant on older Neoglacial moraines than on adjacent younger moraines. Their slow rate of growth makes them a kind of biological clock, and they have been studied for their usefulness as a means of dating these moraines. *Lichenometry* is the technique of ascribing absolute ages to rock substrate by measurement of the maximum diameter of certain lichen species growing on the rocks. The most useful species in the park area are the green crustose lichens *Rhizocarpon geographicum* (Figure 15), for they are slow-

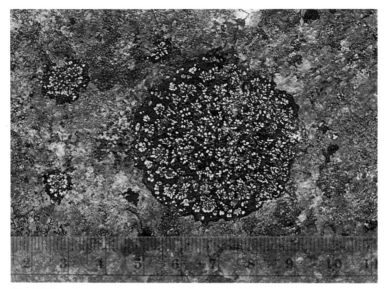

Fig. 15 (above). A forty-five-millimetre-diameter individual of the slow-growing crustose lichen, *Rhizocarpon geographicum.* Individuals of this species may live to be 8,000 years old, and grow to 220 to 280 millimetres in diameter. This particular individual has been growing for about 1,200 years. The scale is in centimetres.

Fig. 16 (opposite, above). An individual of the faster growing lichen, *Alectoria minuscula.* This species is the first colonizer of freshly exposed rock, but is displaced by other species after a few hundred years. The scale is in centimetres.

Fig. 17 (opposite, below). Growth curves showing the increase in diameter with time for the two most useful lichens in the park. The top time-scale refers to the *Alectoria minuscula* curve, while the lower time-scale is for the longer-lived *Rhizocarpon geographicum* curve.

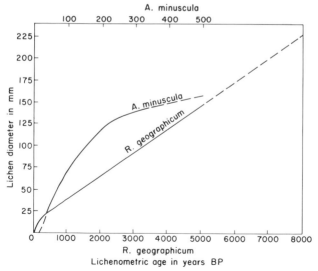

Lichenometric age in years BP

growing, abundant, and among the earliest colonizers of fresh rock surfaces. Although they grow most rapidly during their initial growth period, by the time they reach twenty to twenty-five millimetres (about one inch) in diameter when the rate of growth decreases, they are already 400 years old. After this point they grow more slowly at a steady rate of approximately three millimetres diameter increase per century (about one inch every 1,000 years). The largest individuals of this species are 200 to 280 millimetres (eight and one-half to eleven inches) in diameter and are among the world's oldest living organisms, having lived between 8,000 and 10,000 years! In general practice, lichenometry is most useful on moraines less than 3,500 years old, as on older deposits competition from other plants may curtail growth of the original colonizers. However, the largest lichen always provides an estimate of the minimum age of the deposit. An example of this method may readily be seen by hikers in Pangnirtung Pass. Windy Glacier, in southern Pangnirtung Pass, has formed a massive terminal and lateral moraine complex, and several distinct crests are preserved on the up-valley side. The inner crests, closest to the glacier, are essentially lichen free, indicating that the moraine has stabilized only in the last fifty or so years, whereas on the outer crest *Rhizocarpon geographicum* individuals up to twenty-five millimetres in diameter are present, implying the moraine here was formed more than 400 years ago. Similar examples may be found on other Neoglacial moraines throughout the park.

The other common lichen on Neoglacial moraines is the black "fuzzy" lichen *Alectoria minuscula* (Figure 16). It is also one of the pioneer colonizers, but with a diameter increase of one millimetre per year (roughly one inch every twenty-five years) it grows much faster than the crustose species and disappears after a short life of only 200 to 400 years. The curves showing the increase in lichen diameter with age for these species are shown in Figure 17. Both lichen species are common and easy to identify, and park visitors may use these curves to estimate the ages of Neoglacial deposits on which they are hiking.

Neoglacial Deposits in the Park

Neoglacial moraines are invariably *ice-cored*, and their massive appearance is misleading in terms of the actual volume of rock debris in the moraine. In general, the moraines are composed of only one to three metres of superficial till overlying an ice-core of remnant glacial ice. The superficial debris, once concentrated beyond a critical thickness, acts as an insulating agent for the underlying ice and reduces further melting of the ice-core to near zero, whereas the unprotected glacier ice melts more rapidly. Thus the largest lichen on a Neoglacial moraine probably began growing after the particular glacial advance which formed the moraine had ended, and the superficial till had been sufficiently concentrated that surface boulders were stable and early colonizing lichens could survive.

The earliest recorded Neoglacial advance formed moraines on which the largest *R. geographicum* individuals are now 96 to 102 millimetres in diameter, suggesting an age for the substrate of roughly 3,200 years. As the lichen date is for the warm period after the moraine had been formed, the glacial advance probably occurred somewhat earlier, perhaps about 3,500 years ago. Four subsequent advances are recorded on the peninsula, which terminated prior to 1,650, 800, 400 and 70 years ago (maximum *R. geographicum* on associated moraines are fifty-four, fifty-six, thirty-five, twenty-five and zero to ten millimetres respectively). Of these advances, the most recent was also most extensive, and only in protected localities is evidence for early advances preserved.

Although glaciers are probably the most awesome of the processes currently active in the park, many other agents are also busily involved in modifying the park's landscape. The wind, for example, has always been an important element in the park, particularly in the major valleys and passes where it is channelled by the topography and may reach speeds in excess of 150 kilometres per hour (ninety-five miles per hour). Stones have even been found in Pangnirtung and Kingnait Passes that have been worn down by wind abrasion.

While the wind may erode in some areas, it deposits material in other localities, resulting in extensive accumulations of windblown sands. Unlike sand dunes, these deposits are relatively flat, and were deposited in distinct and nearly horizontal layers, often separated by beds of compressed plant remains. The most extensive of these deposits occur on either side of the Owl River in northern Pangnirtung Pass where they are up to four and one-half metres (fifteen feet) thick, although they also occur elsewhere south of the Penny Ice Cap. Their formation is probably closely associated with glacial activity during the Neoglacial. At the base of the layered sands there is often a thick organic accumulation which may relate to the warm climate following the Late Wisconsin Stade. The oldest date on this material is 6,000 years for plant remains beneath

Fig. 18. Detail of a Neoglacial moraine in the northern part of the park showing that the rock debris (till) is only a metre or two thick, and that the bulk of the moraine is composed of remnant glacial ice. The figure standing at the extreme left centre of the picture provides a scale.

layered sands at the head of North Pangnirtung Fiord. The main layered sand deposit began to accumulate about 2,000 years ago and may be related to an increase in the available sediment which was brought to the pass by the early Neoglacial ice expansions. At present, however, the layered sands are being eroded by both wind and stream action. The wind-blown sands in the pass are mantled by a luxurious growth of vascular plants and the Owl River valley is one of the few places on eastern Baffin Island where grassy slopes dominate over the usual rock rubble.

Elsewhere in the park, deposits of wind-blown debris of less than one metre thickness are common along the valley floors. Although the wind has undoubtedly been active for several millenia, most of the thin wind-blown sand deposits were formed within the past few centuries.

Most of the remaining features in the park which are unique to arctic regions, and with which the visitor may be unfamiliar, are related to the dominant role of the annual freeze/thaw cycle of water. Such features are usually called *periglacial* features, and may be found in northern regions, and in the higher mountains at lower latitudes where the climate begins to approach glacial severity.

Along the base of valley walls, over-steepened and scoured by successive glaciations, large cones of rock debris commonly accumulate. These *talus* or *scree* slopes are accumulations of rocks pried loose from the walls by frost action, and are part of Nature's attempt, little by little, to reduce the steep angle of the valley sides. Talus cones are actively forming throughout the park at present, and these may be extremely unstable. Because the talus slopes accumulate at as steep an angle as the rocks can maintain, disturbance by a hiker may upset the equilibrium and cause the entire slope to move. Consequently, talus should always be crossed with caution. Talus slopes no longer actually accumulating new rocks are mantled by lichens and mosses, and their darker tone contrasts with the fresh lichen-free surface of the active talus cones. Although rocks may be added to the cones at any time, the greatest number arrive during the arctic spring, from late May through early July and during any heavy summer rain. During the time

Fig. 19. A four and one-half metre section of wind-blown sands exposed by a stream cut in northern Pangnirtung Pass. The sands were deposited on top of an old bouldery till within the last 2,000 to 3,000 years, but are being eroded at present.

Fig. 20. A caribou antler protruding beneath forty centimetres of wind-blown sand just below Windy Glacier in southern Pangnirtung Pass. A radiocarbon date on the antler suggests it was buried about 180 years ago.

when snow melt is most intense, the valleys echo the roars of a multitude of snow/debris avalanches which add their rock loads to the talus cones. Most avalanches are generally small, and although major slides do occur, the lichen-free run-out zones are well defined. The main thing to remember when picking a camp spot is that any lichen- or vegetation-free area should be avoided. The lack of vegetation means that some type of disturbance (rockslide, snowslide, flood) probably occurs every year at the locality.

In relatively flat areas, repeated freezing and thawing of moisture in the soil tends to sort the loose material by size, often resulting in some type of pattern displayed at the surface, such as the tundra polygons shown in Figure 23. On gentle slopes, repeated freeze/thaw activity causes superficial material to flow slowly downslope as *solifluction lobes*. When the soil moisture freezes it expands, and causes the soil to rise perpendicular to the slope. When melting occurs, the soil settles vertically under the influence of gravity, resulting in a small net downslope movement each freeze/thaw cycle. Over several thousand years, entire hillslopes of superficial debris may slowly migrate downslope in large solifluction lobes.

Movement of large quantities of loose debris also occurs in *rock glaciers*. Rock glaciers in the park are accumulations of rock debris formed originally either as lateral moraines or talus, and which at some later time began to flow. They have a generally lobate outline, with concentric inner ridges. During cold and/or wet climatic episodes, meltwater percolating through these deposits refreezes in the spaces between the rock debris, until eventually all the spaces are occupied by ice and the deposits, under the influence of gravity, will flow downslope like rock-filled glacier. Active rock glaciers have steep, light-toned (vegetation-free) frontal areas, whereas dormant ones are more rounded and of a uniform dark gray colour.

One peculiar result of the freeze/thaw cycle occurs in fine-grained sediment throughout the park. In these areas, when the water in the sediment expands on freezing in winter, it realigns the finer-grained particles into an expanded framework. When the frozen water melts in spring, the particle structure is rigid enough to remain in its expanded state, and the extra space is taken up by

Fig. 21. Talus cones accumulating at the base of a cliff in northern Pangnirtung Pass. The lack of vegetation on the fresh rocks of the active talus contrasts with the darker-toned vegetation cover on the inactive talus. All talus can be unstable and should be avoided where possible.

Fig. 22. A large snow avalanche which occurred in Narpaing Fiord on July 4, 1970. The run-out zone of slide areas are usually devoid of vegetation and should be avoided as camping areas. A man in the lower photo provides a scale.

Fig. 23. Tundra polygons formed on sandy deposits near the northern end of Kingnait Pass.

more water. If one walks over the deposit, or, better yet, stands in one spot and shifts weight quickly from one foot to the other, the ground soon "turns to jelly" and water oozes out all around. This phenomenon occurs because the realigned particle structure of the sediment is broken down by the vibrations and the sediment compacts, consequently becoming supersaturated with water and turning into a soupy mud.

The whole of Baffin Island lies within the zone of continuous *permafrost*, in which only a thin *active layer* melts during the summer, and at depth the ground remains below freezing throughout the year. In unvegetated sandy areas exposed to the sun, the active layer may be two metres deep, but in finer-grained material, or under thick, mossy vegetation, the active layer may be as little as the upper five to ten centimetres of sediment.

Climate

All of the features discussed above are primarily a result of the response of the physical environment to the various climatic parameters that influence the area. The climate itself, which is really the

Fig. 24. Lobate rock glaciers west of Narpaing Fiord which have flowed toward the centre of the valley. The steep, light-toned front of the rock glacier at the extreme left indicates that it is actively moving at present, whereas the remainder of the rock glaciers are stable. Talus is presently accumulating behind the rock glaciers.

controlling force of both the physical and biological worlds, leaves no direct evidence of its various fluctuations. It is only indirectly, through its manifestations in the response of natural systems that we can detect the nature of past climatic conditions.

Climatic Sensitivity of Baffin Island

One of the most important aspects of Baffin Island is its sensitivity to small-scale climatic fluctuations, due both to its geographical location and proximity to glacial conditions. Many observations from all over the world indicate that average temperatures increased slowly from about 1880 to about 1940 and then decreased from around 1940 to the present. A notable feature of this period is that the regions of greatest warming before 1940 and also of greatest cooling after 1940 have been in higher latitude zones. However, this doesn't necessarily mean that all high latitude areas are warming or cooling simultaneously. Averaged around a line of latitude, temperatures may appear to be cooling but there may also be distinct regional variations. The atmosphere does not operate in simple bands east/west but moves in a series of waves which may be oriented north/south in some sectors (Figure 25). Thus, some areas may be primarily influenced by northerly air flow and other areas may receive air flow from the south, and the extent and frequency of these different cool or warm air masses may vary from day to day, month to month and decade to decade. This is what determines our daily weather, our climate and our changes in climate. It is these changes which most concern us in Auyuittuq National Park.

The wave-like structure of the atmosphere may not be obvious from a look at a daily weather map of the atmospheric circulation at sea level. However, a map of the air movement above the surface (above the disturbing influence of topography—say 5,000 metres), reveals this wave-like motion. Furthermore, certain waves tend to stay in more or less the same position relative to the earth's surface

Fig. 25. Waves in the upper levels of the atmosphere carry cool air towards the equator on their western margins and warm air towards the poles on the eastern margins. Changes in the position of these waves can affect the climate of the area beneath them. Baffin Island is located beneath one of the main waves in the upper atmosphere—a large low pressure wedge or trough—and it is thought that past changes in the climate of the park reflect changes in the position of this trough and hence in the circulation of the atmosphere as a whole.

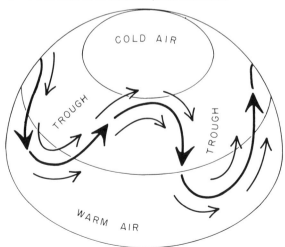

and actually influence the movements of travelling high pressure systems (*anticyclones*) and low pressure systems (*depressions* or *cyclones*) at the surface, systems which are directly responsible for our day to day weather changes.

It so happens that Baffin Island is located directly beneath one of the most important waves in the upper atmosphere: a large low pressure wedge or *trough*. Air flow is predominantly from the northwest on the western side of this trough and from the southeast on the eastern side. Air drawn from these two directions is of course quite different, particularly at times when open water lies in Davis Strait and the Canadian archipelago is choked with ice, as is common in the spring and early summer. Thus, if the position of the trough varies slightly from year to year or decade to decade the climate of Baffin Island will also vary in response to the accompanying change in air flow over the region. Baffin Island is, therefore, in a critical position with regard to this upper air wave which is an important feature of the world's atmospheric circulation as a whole. It is in this sense that we can consider Baffin Island in particular to be a "sensitive" area for studies of climatic change, because it is likely that changes in the upper atmospheric wave structure

Fig. 26. Broughton Harbour choked with pack-ice in September. The movement of near-shore pack-ice is unpredictable, and a good offshore wind could disperse it within a few days.

over the island had a significant impact on its climatic environment and hence its people, wildlife and glaciers.

Although we have shown that small shifts in the atmospheric circulation may substantially influence the climate of the island, these changes must be manifested in the physical or biological environments if we are to decipher past climatic events. Events of the last two decades amply demonstrate the sensitivity of the physical environment in the park to climatic fluctuations. Since about 1950, summer temperatures on Baffin Island have fallen, and at the close of the 1960s average temperatures were cooler than they had been for the preceding thirty to forty years. This is the result of more fre-

Fig. 27. The extent of sea ice in August and September during (a) the 1950s and (b) the 1960s. Between 1952 and 1960 there were only four years when significant areas of ice were observed in September, whereas in the 1960s there was only one year in which ice *was not* present in September and five years when it survived into October! This reflects the lower temperatures and increase in northerly air flow over the region in the 1960s. Available data indicate similar conditions in the early 1970s. The changes have been of major significance to hunting and movement along the east coast where persistent ice delays travel by boat. In 1972, for example, the Inuit on Broughton Island were able to greet the sea-lift (in late August) by snowmobile rather than by canoe!

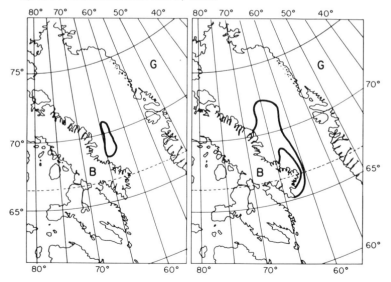

quent outbreaks of cool northerly air flow over the region in recent years, a condition which has also had important consequences for sea-ice in the area (Figure 27). What is more, during the 1960s in particular, there was a marked rise in winter temperatures (though still averaging well below freezing) and this has been accompanied by increased snowfall over the island. This is thought to be the result of warmer, moister air being carried north in the winter, leading to more moisture available for precipitation. The overall result has been more snow falling, and less melting in summer months—conditions approaching those of the "little ice age", but less severe. Although this latest episode is relatively recent, it has been noticed that some areas which were free of snow in 1949 already had permanent snowbanks in the late 1960s. In addition, many inland lakes which were ice-free by early August in the 1950s and early 1960s, have remained ice-covered throughout the summers in recent years. Such marked changes in the landscape of the park over extremely short intervals clearly reflect the sensitivity of the area to small climatic changes, and emphasize their importance in providing records of climatic events of the past. Indeed, this fact was noted many years ago by Ralph Tarr who in 1896, while on a journey to join Admiral Peary in northern Greenland, made the following observation about Cumberland Peninsula:

> "So far as I can estimate from my short visit, it seems there must be places not far above the sea level where even now the snow stays throughout the summer. A slight change in climate is all that is needed to increase the number of these and to add to their area and depth. . . . the climatic conditions of Baffin Land and Labrador are wonderfully near those which produce glaciation."

Reconstructing Past Climates

What, then, are the most useful climatically dependent phenomena from which we can reconstruct the climate of the past? Glaciers are certainly one such feature. The growth of glaciers and small ice caps will occur if, over several decades, the snow *accumulation* exceeds the snow melt (*ablation*). While excess snowfall continues, glaciers will slowly advance downslope, carrying with them rock material eroded from the base and sides of the ice to form moraines. When the climate reverts to warmer conditions, where more ablation occurs than accumulation, glaciers will recede, leaving their former margins outlined by the rocky moraines. Hence, the positions of moraines are related to changes in glacier sizes, which, in turn, are the result of changes in climate.

Another way of reconstructing past climates is through the study of pollen grains (*palynology*). Pollen grains produced by flowering plants are extremely resistant to decay, and in suitable environments can survive intact for many thousands of years. By looking at the relative numbers of different kinds of pollen accumulated over time, it is possible to reconstruct the vegetation at different periods in the past, and thereby make some general statements about the climate at those times. Such an approach assumes that certain vegetation types are restricted to areas with particular types of climate. If, for example, large amounts of spruce pollen were found on Baffin Island, this might be interpreted to mean that the climate at the time the pollen accumulated was similar to the climate of northern Quebec or Labrador today.

A similar technique has been developed using marine molluscs which inhabit the coastal waters of Cumberland Peninsula. Many species are restricted to waters of a certain temperature, and variations in the number of different species can be used to infer water temperatures and hence to indicate broad scale climatic conditions.

These three techniques have been the principal tools used in the park to reconstruct and understand climates of the past. However, the farther back in time one goes, the more difficult it becomes to assess the actual climatic conditions, as it is more likely that the material on which the studies are carried out have been disturbed (or in many cases destroyed) by later events—rock slides, flooding, burial by sand dunes, and so on. Therefore, we know more about the most recent period of Baffin's climatic history (the last 10,000 years) than we do about earlier periods.

Climatic Flucuations in Historical and Recent Times

The first known meteorological observations on Baffin Island were made less than 100 years ago on the shores of Cumberland Sound. In 1881, a German expedition wintered over at the head of the Sound as part of the first International Polar Year. Much was learned about the climate of the area as a result of their observations over the year, but no permanent weather stations were maintained on Baffin Island until the early 1920s (at Pangnirtung and Lake Harbour, on southwestern Baffin). Hence direct observations of weather and climate in the park area cover only a relatively short period. In spite of this, a general picture of climate over the

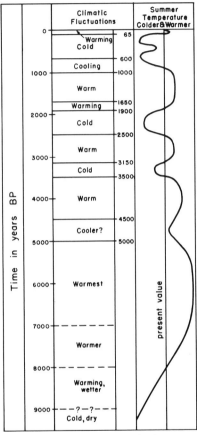

Fig. 28. Climatic fluctuations during the last 9,000 years. At the last glacial maximum, Cumberland Peninsula was very cold and dry, but became warmer and wetter as the glacial episode waned. Maximum temperatures were probably reached between 7,000 and 5,000 years ago, with a minimum distribution of glacial ice about 5,000 years ago. Since then, summer temperatures have been cooler. About 3,500 years ago, summer temperatures dropped below present values, initiating the Neoglacial. Glacial advances occurred when summer temperatures were below normal; glaciers were smallest during episodes of warm summers. Human migrations into the eastern Arctic coincided with periods of relative warmth (about 3,500-4,000 and around 1,000 years ago).

past 300 to 400 years has been compiled through other lines of evidence and meteorological data from other parts of the world.

There are many records from western Europe and Iceland of a cool damp period beginning about 1600 and lasting to about 1850 A.D. During this period, the so-called "little ice age", crop failures were common, glaciers in Europe and North America advanced and pack-ice in the North Atlantic was very extensive, frequently reaching as far south as Iceland. The cooler, damper, more stormy conditions appear to have been global or at least hemispheric in extent and the period is recorded clearly in the landscape of Auyuittuq National Park. During this period, extensive areas of the Baffin Island plateau around the Barnes Ice Cap (north of the park) and parts of Cumberland Peninsula became snow covered, killing lichens and other vegetation growing on the underlying surface. In recent years, probably within the last fifty to 100 years, these areas have become snow-free again, but the extent of the former snowbanks can still be seen by the areas of *lichen-kill*. Throughout the park, these light-toned areas, often surrounding present day snowbanks, indicate the former more extensive snow cover during the "little ice age".

Another result of the "little ice age" was the growth of glaciers throughout the park. We can surmise that the "average" summer of this period was similar to the worst summers of today (such as those in 1970, 1972); cloudy and cool (temperatures probably only reaching the low forties Fahrenheit on the best of days) with frequent snowy periods throughout the summer. Snowfall in winter months was also probably heavier, with the result that more snow fell on the land and less melted off in the summer. These conditions naturally favoured the "health" of Baffin ice bodies and eventually glaciers began to advance, carrying with them eroded material to form new systems of moraines. In fact, most glaciers advanced further than they had for 5,000 to 6,000 years and a few actually reached the position they had attained at the height of the last major glacial episode (the late Wisconsin).

Towards the middle of the last century, the "little ice age" period came to an end. We really do not know why this happened, though we should be thankful that it did; a continuation of the climate conditions might well have led to a full-scale glaciation similar to that which resulted in the burial of continental North America beneath the vast Laurentide Ice Sheet. At any rate, there was a turn for the better about 100 years ago and average temperatures began to rise in most parts of the world. We have direct evidence of this from records kept on the opposite side of Davis Strait—at Upernavik and Jacobshavn on the west coast of Greenland. These records indicate that summer temperatures increased by one and one-half to two degrees Celsius from 1880 to 1940, and winter temperatures rose by four to five degrees Celsius during the same period. As a result of this change to milder conditions (particularly in summer months) glaciers in the park began to recede once more, and today virtually all glaciers on Baffin Island are receding in response to the warming period between 1880 and 1940.

Although the climatic deterioration of the last decade has caused snowbanks to expand and a longer duration of ice cover on the lakes and ocean, this does not necessarily mean that glacier advances are imminent; even during this recent trend towards glacierization, an occasional warm summer may obliterate the small accumulation gains made on the glaciers in previous years. Only if the present trend continues for a relatively long period of time (perhaps for another two or more decades) can we expect to see signs of glacial advance. However, in view of the fact that the last glaciation probably began on Baffin Island it is obviously very important that we continue careful monitoring of glacial activity in the park.

Weather Conditions in the Park

Anybody who has visited Baffin Island over a number of years will be well aware that summer weather can vary dramatically from one year to the next. If you had visited the park in the "summer" of 1970 or 1972 you might have been excused for not wanting to visit the area again! Both summers were cold, snowy and cloudy with only a few days in July that varied noticeably. However, other summers may be spectacularly different—sunny, relatively warm and with only a little snow (for example, the summer of 1974). This characteristic year-to-year variability of Baffin weather should be remembered when considering the following *average* statistics (see Tables I to V and Figures 29 to 33).

Only five weather stations are presently operated in and around the park—at Pangnirtung, Cape Dyer, Broughton Island, Cape Hooper and Dewar Lakes. Of these, Cape Dyer is somewhat anomalous due to the occurrence off the coast of persistent ice-free areas for much of the year, resulting in much heavier precipitation in that area than anywhere else on Cumberland Peninsula. Figures 29 to 33 show average monthly temperatures and precipitation totals at the five main stations. Three of these operated throughout the 1960s but the Pangnirtung station has records only for the 1930s when climatic conditions may have been quite different from those in the 1960s (see above). Also the Pangnirtung observations are the only ones taken close to sea level—all the others are taken at heights of 350 metres (1,200 feet) or more above sea level. Bearing these facts in mind we can make some generalizations about the usual summer weather conditions and also the extremes one may encounter during a visit to the park.

Over most of the region monthly average temperatures at the height of the summer are generally in the five to eight degrees Celsius range (low to mid forties Fahrenheit). Average daily maximum temperatures range from eight to eleven degrees Celsius (forty-six to fifty-two degrees Fahrenheit). However, these averages disguise the extremes which may occur; during the 1960s, lowest July temperatures were around minus five degrees Celsius (low twenties Fahrenheit) and one can expect a frost on one day in three or four, even at the height of the summer. On the other hand, maximum temperatures on some days may reach twenty degrees Celsius (sixty-eight degrees Fahrenheit) and a record high of twenty-six degrees Celsius (eighty degrees Fahrenheit) was recorded on one balmy day at Pangnirtung in the 1930s.

Rain and snow may fall at any time of the year (indeed, at times one feels that it falls *all* the year!) but highest amounts generally occur in late summer and fall (mid-August to mid-November—see Figures 29 to 33). Even in July, five centimetres (two inches) or more of snow in twenty-four hours has been recorded at several stations. However, snow may be less of a problem to park visitors than the occasional heavy downpour of rain; two and one-half centimetres (one inch) of rain in twenty-four hours is not beyond the bounds of possibility, particularly in August. One can expect an average of one or two days a week with some form of precipitation (rain, snow or sleet) even at the height of the summer, so if you spend a week or ten days in the park without any rain or snow you can consider yourself very fortunate!

Perhaps the most important aspect of Baffin weather and climate is not just its year-to-year variation but also its variability from one area to another. The orientation of the valleys, amount of shading, and the proximity to ice bodies and open water can all greatly affect the local or *topoclimate*. Particularly striking is the climatic gradient which frequently develops between the fiord mouths along the eastern coast and the fiord heads twenty to fifty kilometres inland. By early July, frequent overcast conditions or persistent fogs along the coastal margins may delay snow-melt, whereas further inland the more frequent sunny periods lead to earlier snowfree conditions. Local open water conditions can be extremely significant in maintaining dense fogs along the coast by providing the extra moisture necessary for condensation to take place.

Another important topoclimatic effect is the effect of topography itself on funnelling air in certain fixed directions. This may result in persistent windy conditions and increased wind chill in some localized areas while elsewhere the air is relatively calm. The drainage of cold air down valleys under the influence of gravity can also lead to "frost-pockets" or pools of very cold air in valley bottoms. This is an example of a *temperature inversion* where the coldest air is closest to the ground and temperatures increase with elevation instead of decreasing. It is not uncommon for this cooler air to be "saturated", that is, to form a layer of fog or low stratus cloud. Some of the most memorable views of the park occur when one looks out from a hilltop over a vast sea of fog filling the valleys, with only the mountain summits emerging in all their magnificent splendour from the gloom below.

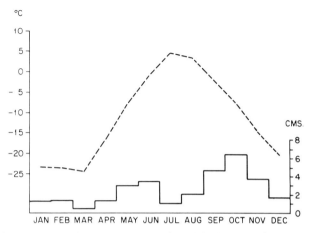

Fig. 29. Average monthly temperatures and precipitation totals (rain, melted snow and sleet) for Broughton Island (1961-70).

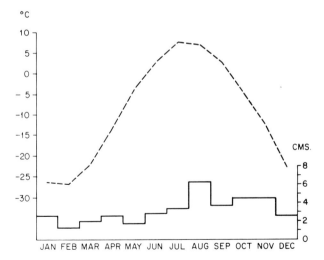

Fig. 30. Average monthly temperature and precipitation totals (rain, melted snow and sleet) for Pangnirtung (1931-40).

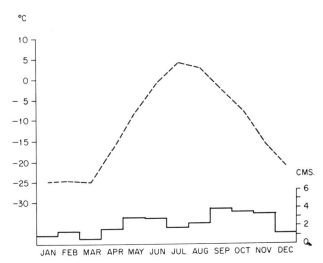

Fig. 31. Average monthly temperatures and precipitation totals (rain, melted snow and sleet) for Cape Hooper (1961-70).

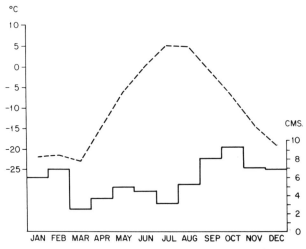

Fig. 32. Average monthly temperatures and precipitation totals (rain, melted snow and sleet) for Cape Dyer (1961-70).

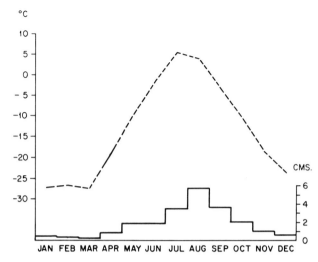

Fig. 33. Average monthly temperatures and precipitation totals (rain, melted snow and sleet) for Dewar Lakes (1961-70).

Climatic records for the five permanent weather stations closest to the park.

Table I Broughton Island (580 m)

	Jan.	Feb.	Mar.	Apr.	May	June	July	Aug.	Sept.	Oct.	Nov.	Dec.	Annual
Average daily maximum temperature (°C)	−21	−22	−20	−14	−4	2	8	6	0	−6	−12	−19	−8
Average daily minimum temperature (°C)	−27	−28	−27	−20	−10	−3	2	1	−4	−10	−18	−24	−14
Extreme maximum temperature (°C) (12 year record)	0	2	−2	6	7	15	18	18	14	7	3	5	18
Extreme minimum temperature (°C) (13 year record)	−42	−40	−39	−33	−26	−12	−6	−6	−12	−21	−31	−37	−42
Number of days with frost	31	28	31	30	31	27	12	16	27	31	30	31	325
Greatest precipitation in 24 hours (centimetres)	3.2	1.4	0.7	2.3	2.0	3.6	1.0	2.6	3.3	3.8	3.3	2.2	3.8
Number of days with measurable precipitation	4	5	3	4	10	7	4	5	10	11	8	5	76

Table II Cape Dyer (375 m)

	Jan.	Feb.	Mar.	Apr.	May	June	July	Aug.	Sept.	Oct.	Nov.	Dec.	Annual
Average daily maximum temperature (°C)	−18	−18	−18	−10	−2	4	9	8	2	−4	−11	−16	−6
Average daily minimum temperature (°C)	−27	−28	−27	−19	−9	−3	2	1	−4	−11	−19	−25	−14
Extreme maximum temperature (°C) (11 year record)	1	2	1	3	8	13	19	19	16	9	3	6	19
Extreme minimum temperature (°C) (11 year record)	−43	−42	−47	−33	−28	−14	−4	−5	−19	−25	−39	−44	−47
Number of days with frost	31	28	31	30	31	26	10	11	26	31	30	31	316
Greatest precipitation in 24 hours (centimetres)	4.0	4.8	5.5	3.4	2.5	3.7	3.8	4.4	5.2	8.0	3.5	4.1	8.0
Number of days with measurable precipitation	11	12	7	9	13	11	8	11	13	16	13	12	136

−40°C = −40°F, −20°C = −4°F, 0°C = 32°F, 10°C = 50°F, 20°C = 68°F
1 cm = 0.4 inches, 2.5 cm = 1 inch
30 m = about 100 ft.

Table III Cape Hooper (400 m)

	Jan.	Feb.	Mar.	Apr.	May	June	July	Aug.	Sept.	Oct.	Nov.	Dec.	Annual
Average daily maximum temperature (°C)	−22	−23	−21	−14	−5	2	8	5	0	−6	−13	−19	−9
Average daily minimum temperature (°C)	−28	−28	−27	−20	−10	−3	2	1	−3	−9	−18	−24	−14
Extreme maximum temperature (°C) (14 year record)	−2	−1	−2	1	11	18	19	17	13	5	2	3	19
Extreme minimum temperature (°C) (14 year record)	−41	−39	−41	−34	−28	−9	−7	−6	−12	−25	−26	−41	−41
Number of days with frost	31	28	29	30	31	27	13	19	27	31	30	31	327
Greatest precipitation in 24 hours (centimetres)	2.3	2.2	1.5	2.3	1.9	3.3	2.0	2.6	1.9	2.5	2.4	2.3	3.3
Number of days with measurable precipitation	4	6	3	5	8	6	5	8	10	10	9	6	80

Table IV Dewar Lakes (518 m)

	Jan.	Feb.	Mar.	Apr.	May	June	July	Aug.	Sept.	Oct.	Nov.	Dec.	Annual
Average daily maximum temperature (°C)	-24	-24	-23	-16	-6	2	9	7	-1	-8	-16	-22	-10
Average daily minimum temperature (°C)	-30	-31	-30	-22	-11	-3	3	1	-5	-13	-22	-27	-16
Extreme maximum temperature (°C) (13 year record)	-3	0	-3	-1	6	12	20	21	11	3	-1	-1	21
Extreme minimum temperature (°C) (13 year record)	-47	-46	-48	-39	-29	-17	-3	-7	-17	-30	-41	-45	-48
Number of days with frost	31	28	31	30	31	26	8	13	28	31	30	31	318
Greatest precipitation in 24 hours (centimetres)	0.7	1.1	1.0	1.4	2.0	1.9	3.6	4.6	2.2	1.0	1.1	1.1	4.6
Number of days with measurable precipitation	2	2	1	4	7	6	7	7	9	8	4	2	59

-40°C = -40°F, -20°C = -4°F, 0°C = 32°F, 10°C = 50°F, 20°C = 68°F
1 cm = 0.4 inches, 2.5 cm = 1 inch
30 m = about 100 ft.

Table V Pangnirtung (13 m)

	Jan.	Feb.	Mar.	Apr.	May	June	July	Aug.	Sept.	Oct.	Nov.	Dec.	Annual
Average daily maximum temperature (°C)	−23	−23	−17	−8	1	6	11	10	6	−1.1	−8	−18	−6
Average daily minimum temperature (°C)	−30	−31	−26	−17	−7	0	4	4	1	−7	−14	−25	−12
Extreme maximum temperature (°C) (11 year record)	9	3	6	11	15	21	27	19	17	13	11	12	27
Extreme minimum temperature (°C) (11 year record)	−43	−43	−43	−36	−26	−6	−1	−1	−11	−17	−30	−41	−43
Number of days with frost					— No data available —								
Greatest precipitation in 24 hours (centimetres)	1.3	3.7	2.0	1.5	1.4	2.9	2.5	3.8	3.7	3.1	2.3	3.1	3.8
Number of days with measurable precipitation	6	3	4	6	4	7	9	11	8	8	8	5	79

−40 °C = −40 °F, −20 °C = −4 °F, 0 °C = 32 °F, 10 °C = 50 °F, 20 °C = 68 °F
1 cm = 0.4 inches, 2.5 cm = 1 inch
30 m = about 100 ft.

References

Geology

Baird, David M. *A Guide to Geology.* Ottawa: Dept. of Indian and Northern Affairs and Parks Canada, 1974.

An inexpensive guidebook for visitors to Canada's National Parks. An easy-to-read yet informative textbook of geology.

Flint, Richard F. *Glacial and Quaternary Geology.* New York: John Wiley & Sons, 1971.

An updated and thorough treatment of the history of our planet during the last two to three million years. The "standard" text for college courses in glacial geology.

Geology and Economic Minerals of Canada. Ottawa: Dept. of Energy, Mines and Resources, 1970.

The most comprehensive single volume on the geology of Canada: produced by the Geological Survey of Canada and somewhat technical. Available at Information Canada bookstores for $12. A supplementary volume containing charts and maps is also available, including the Glacial Map of Canada.

Paterson, W.S. *The Physics of Glaciers.* Oxford: Pergamon Press, 1969.

A comprehensive (and at times very technical) treatment of all aspects of glacial studies: how glaciers form, how and why they flow, and the complex relationship between meteorological parameters and their effects on glaciers.

Climate

Calder, N. *The Weather Machine.* London: B.B.C., 1974.

A popular account of climatic change with speculations on causes and what the future may hold in store for us.

Hare, F.K. and Thomas, M.K. *Climate Canada*. Toronto: John Wiley & Sons, 1974.

The authoritative work on Canada's climate with a chapter on climatic change.

Ladurie, E. LeRoy. *Times of Feast, Times of Famine: A History of Climate Since the Year 1000*. New York: Doubleday, 1971.

A fascinating account of the impact that climatic fluctuations have had over the last thousand years on agriculture, wine production, glaciers and life in western Europe.

Lamb, H.H. *The Changing Climate: Papers on Climatic Variations*. London: Methuen, 1966.

A collection of studies of climatic change by the world's leading authority.

Acknowledgements

Much of the impetus for the recent research into the glacial history of Cumberland Peninsula is due to Dr. John Andrews, Associate Director of the Institute of Arctic and Alpine Research at the University of Colorado. His encouragement and active participation in all phases of the research has been important, as has his love of the Arctic. Mal Anderson, who also shares this love, has provided companionship and assistance during five summers of geological studies; many other students of arctic geology have contributed their ideas and data to this project as well. Ernie Sieber, Operations Manager of Auyuittuq National Park, enthusiastically supported the idea of a book on the park from our earliest discussions of the project. Credit is also due to the early explorers and scientists, many of whom endured greater hardships than most of us will ever know to lay the framework for our later studies of the arctic regions.

2. History of Human Occupation

Peter Schledermann

Following the gradual retreat of the Laurentide ice sheet, the vast geographical regions of northern North America slowly began to support an increasing number of life forms. A long and complex series of events preceded the advance of human populations into this area.

The interaction between human cultures and a variety of environmental habitats goes back over a million years in the Old World. Culture is the sum total of all learned and shared traits of a human society, a buffer between the individual and the environment. Through inventions and transmitted knowledge, the early human groups increased their adaptability to changing environmental zones, expanding the geographical extent of their domain. Eventually some of these cultures spread into northeast Asia and the New World. The time period for this last event is still a much debated question, but it is probably safe to assume that it took place at least 40,000 years ago, at which time the North American and Asian continents were connected by a landbridge, between Alaska and Siberia, called Beringia.

These early wanderers were the ancestors of the present-day Indians, and while the Wisconsin ice sheets still covered most of northern North America, their cultures advanced and diversified throughout the remaining regions of the New World.

The interplay between culture and environment is a continuing process, unique in every case because of the diversity of habitats and cultural manifestations. The environment modifies and to some degree shapes the culture which in turn may modify and shape the environment. Throughout most of his existence, man survived as a hunter and gatherer. The confrontation between the social group and nature was direct and the primary focus was on obtaining food. Among many so-called "primitive" bands, gathering, usually the work of women and children, comprised the major source of food during the year. Seasonal movements and migrations were usually determined by the changing availability of food sources. Mobility was a matter of survival often dictating a limit to the numbers of material possessions which could be transferred from one place to the next. When the economic life of a band was based on hunting as well as gathering, the survival factor was greatly enhanced. Failure in one area could be compensated for by increased activity in the other. In cases where the pursuit of game provided the only means of subsistence, survival often became a doubtful proposition.

By modern standards, such cultural groups apparently existed under the constant threat of starvation and privation. Although such threats were no doubt occasionally realized, what we tend to ignore is that the precarious conditions under which these people lived were perceived and accepted by them as an integral part of life.

The man/land relationship sets up an intriguing process in which man is continually trying to gain a greater control over his destiny. The first effective attempts at domesticating plants and animals began "only" about 8,000 years ago and the ability to secure and maintain an available food supply throughout the year brought about a more sedentary existence for an increasing number of people. This cultural development formed the basis for the emergence of modern existence.

Whereas a number of different cultures took part in this innovation in the Old as well as the New World, many other cultural groups remained beyond its reach, continuing their patterns of hunting and gathering. In the more northerly regions, plant domestication was ruled out by climate and most of the northern cultures in America based their economic existence on hunting and fishing. Collecting played a very small part in the seasonal subsistence cycle. Animal domestication was possible to some extent, confined primarily to reindeer herding by a number of northern people in the

Old World. This cultural development, as far as we know, was not transmitted to the New World until fairly recently, and to date the experiment has been only partially successful in the north. Cultures are usually quite conservative and resistant to major change. After all, if things are going well, why take a chance?

We have come to know the Inuit people and admire their cultural adaptation to an unpredictable and often harsh environment. This well-founded admiration, however, tends to emphasize the differences between our culture and theirs. Prior to white contact the Inuit culture was self-contained, whereas ours was, and still is, dependent upon a complex system of trade and communication networks. The Norse colonization period in Greenland is an early example of that dependence and clearly illustrates the most likely outcome of cutting the life-line with the parent culture. Political and climatic events reduced the trade contacts between the colonizers and European merchants, and although the Norsemen had existed on the Greenlandic coast for centuries, their cultural heritage did not enable them to adopt an independent life-style suitable to an isolated life. Cultural isolation, as well as increasing competition with the advancing Inuit of the Thule culture, coincided with a deteriorating climate period, all of which proved too much for the Norsemen. After almost 500 years of settlement in southeastern Greenland they died out, relinquishing the land to a people whose culture was well adapted to a self-sustained existence.

Discovering the Past

Archaeological research in the arctic regions of North America has progressed very slowly. Large geographical regions have yet to be investigated and many questions are still unanswered. Transportation to remote regions, a short working season and frozen ground conditions are some of the difficulties facing the prehistorian. The recent increasing human destruction of archaeological sites is adding to the dilemma.

One of the most important aims of archaeological research is to construct a history of past cultural events, often based upon a limited amount of material evidence. To do this the prehistorian cannot rely on existing records but must piece together the evidence produced by careful excavation and recording of old settlements and encampments.

Often it is the refuse left behind by past cultures which enables the researcher to reconstruct cultural activities in a particular area.

Such refuse areas, also called middens, may have accumulated over a long period of time and consist of many layers of cultural evidence. A site that has been inhabited by several successive cultural groups is said to be multi-component. Layer by layer the locations of all findings are carefully noted and the progress of the excavation recorded by photographs and scaled drawings. These records are an invaluable help in the later laboratory reconstruction when all the little pieces of evidence are put together. Inadequate preservation of material is a great obstacle encountered at many sites and the investigator may be left with nothing but stone tools. Despite these difficulties, however, enough information can often be acquired from a site to suggest its relationship to other areas. The multi-component sites are particularly useful in the attempt to establish cultural chronologies. Ideally, the lower levels will represent the earlier cultures and the upper levels the later habitation periods of the site. Sometimes a sterile (non-cultural) layer of deposits separates the components, indicating a period when a particular site was not used.

House structures and other cultural features are recorded and excavated with the same care. The archaeologist is aware that once a site has been excavated, it is essentially destroyed. He or she must therefore ensure that all information that can possibly be gained from the area has been recorded in such a way that a reconstruction of the site is possible, at least on paper. All the artifacts are numbered and described individually on special cards which also indicate the precise location of each find. Special preservation techniques are often employed in order to keep excavated speciments from disintegrating. This is particularly important in the case of wooden or bone artifacts which may have been frozen for centuries prior to excavation. The frozen ground conditions are both an advantage and a disadvantage to the excavator. The preservation of cultural materials is usually quite good, but the work proceeds very slowly depending upon the daily rate of thawing.

By training, many archaeologists are also good cultural observers who can combine their knowledge of present-day hunting activities, for example, with a study of maps and aerial photos in the search for prehistoric settlement locations. In the north the prehistorian is often aided in his investigations by the older people and active hunters in a community when these people know that the aim of his work is to bring to light their own cultural heritage.

Obviously, a disturbed archaeological site is of little value to the prehistorian who can then no longer be certain of the original context of the cultural material. Museums are full of collections that lack good locational data, and although the material is interesting enough for display purposes, it is of limited use to the archaeologist. The importance of precise locational data is not confined only to the material artifacts; if the bone refuse is mixed, very little can be determined regarding possible changes in the economic pursuits of the people through time.

Although there are regulations which make it a punishable offence to tamper with sites of archaeological, ethnological or historical importance, such laws are difficult to enforce. The preservation of this great northern heritage must finally depend on the people who live in and visit the area.

Inuit Origins

There are a number of theories regarding the origins of Inuit culture, the elaborations of which are too involved for the purpose of this chapter. Following one line of thought, it may be postulated that the Bering Landbridge, connecting Alaska and Siberia, supported two cultural traditions towards the end of the last major glacial period (Figure 34). One of these traditions consisted of a maritime-adapted people who occupied the coastal regions of Beringia. The second culture was adapted to a life in the forest, tundra and grassland environment of the interior regions. With the gradual submergence of the landbridge, as the ice sheets melted and the sea level rose, these two traditions began to share a number of traits which eventually influenced some of the cultural developments along the west coast of Alaska. It appears that some of the interior groups began to spend at least parts of the year on the coast, and by about 4,500 years ago a cultural tradition known as the Arctic Small Tool tradition was well established in the region. Although they exploited the coastal regions, these people still maintained a strong inland-oriented hunting economy. Their culture was well adapted to life on the tundra and the arctic coast. The term "Arctic Small Tool" (which will be abbreviated to A.S.T.) refers to the minuscule stone implements used by the people of this culture (Figure 35). The stone tools show a high degree of delicate workmanship and an almost artistic level of flaking techniques.

While the cultures in the Bering Strait regions gradually developed a stronger maritime orientation, groups of the A.S.T. people wandered eastward into the Canadian Arctic. They are considered by many prehistorians to have been essentially Eskimoid

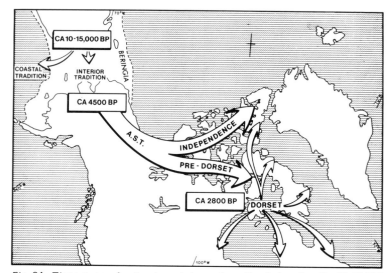

Fig. 34. Three stages of cultural events in northern North America: Ca. 10-15,000 BP, the presence of two major cultural traditions in northeast Asia, Beringia and parts of Alaska; Ca. 4,500 BP, the landbridge was submerged and people of the A.S.T. culture migrated into the Canadian Arctic; Ca. 2,800 BP, the development of the Dorset culture in the central Arctic. This event is much debated by arctic prehistorians and there are several different interpretations. The Dorset culture most probably developed out of Pre-Dorset with the possible addition of cultural traits from northern Indian cultures.

and have been termed variously Paleo- and Proto-Eskimos. Unfortunately we do not have any skeletal material from the early period of the A.S.T. culture which would clarify this point.

Archaeological investigations to date suggest that one of these early Paleo-Eskimo groups, the Independence I people (the name derives from the Independence Fiord region in northeast Greenland where their cultural remains were first recognized), originally followed the so-called "musk-ox way" through the Arctic Islands into northern Greenland. As indicated by the name of this migration route, musk oxen were probably fairly numerous and it is generally believed that the Independence I people utilized these animals as a primary food source. Because of their particular tendency to crowd together in a circular defence formation, these animals were probably not difficult to hunt, in fact musk ox hunting may have been too easy. Indications are that these animals were not able to survive prolonged human hunting pressures, a factor which may have encouraged further human migrations in search of new hunting areas. As far as we know, the Independence I people remained primarily in the high arctic regions in both Canada and Greenland, and a number of radiocarbon dates suggests that the initial occupation in these areas took place towards the end of the climatic optimum about 4,000 years ago. No traces of lamps for light, heat and cooking have been found and it is assumed that these people managed with whatever driftwood and local willow they could find. Their dwellings were probably skin-covered tent structures secured to the ground by a ring of boulders. The structures were divided in the centre by a slab-lined passage which contained a fire hearth and storage compartments. Looking at the remains of these small structures today, it is difficult to understand how the inhabitants could have survived for any length of time the rigours of one of the most inhospitable climates in the world.

Another group of Paleo-Eskimos, the Pre-Dorset people, moved into the central and eastern Arctic from the west at about the same time. A great deal of additional research is needed to determine with certainty the complex relationship between these two early

Fig. 35. Tools of the A.S.T. tradition from the park area. *Top left to right:* two burins, crescent-shaped blade for inset in bone or antler, "knife" blade. *Bottom left to right:* three stone points (centre point an early Dorset variety), microblade.

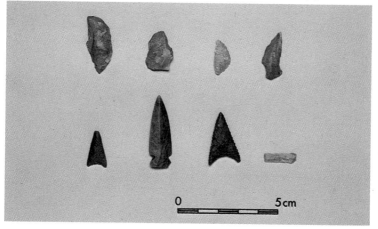

cultures or phases of the A.S.T. tradition. Two important material
items appear in early Pre-Dorset sites—the toggle harpoon head
and the stone lamp. The harpoon heads, which were used for sea
mammal hunting, are some of the best indicators of cultural affinities as well as time markers in prehistoric Eskimo research. Each
harpoon head exhibits a number of attributes which have changed
significantly through time. Some of the important attributes are noted on the illustration (Figure 36) of an early Pre-Dorset harpoon
head found near Igloolik, west of Baffin Island. The trained prehistorian can, with a fair degree of accuracy, determine the cultural af-
filiation and age of a particular harpoon head. On an undisturbed
site, the location of this cultural item is therefore of the greatest importance as it will aid in the temporal placement of other less distinctive material specimens.

The Pre-Dorset people were present in the park area approximately 3,500 years ago. This early phase of the A.S.T. tradition
has been investigated extensively along the south coast of Baffin Island, Frobisher Bay, and in the vicinity of Pond Inlet; however,
evidence concerning these people is still very limited in the Cumberland Peninsula regions, and is mostly confined to a small number of scattered hunting camps along the coast.

The tool inventory of the A.S.T. people included a very important tool-making tool called a burin (Figure 37), which was used as a

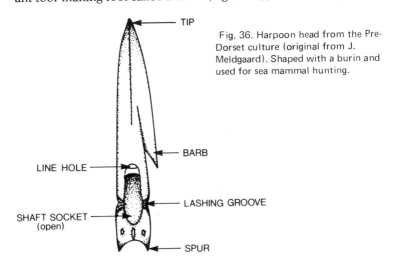

TIP

BARB

LINE HOLE

LASHING GROOVE

SHAFT SOCKET
(open)

SPUR

Fig. 36. Harpoon head from the Pre-
Dorset culture (original from J.
Meldgaard). Shaped with a burin and
used for sea mammal hunting.

Fig. 37. Burin (made of chert) from the A.S.T. tradition. When the working edge of the tip of the burin became too worn, a burin spall was detached in order to create a new sharp edge. The burin was probably set in a bone handle and in some cases the burin spall itself was hafted and used as a cutting tool.

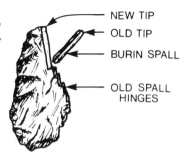

NEW TIP
OLD TIP
BURIN SPALL
OLD SPALL HINGES

grooving and incising instrument. Harpoon heads and lance heads were shaped out of bone, ivory or antler, with the aid of the burin. A slow process no doubt, but one which has given a very distinct character to the bone, antler and ivory tools of that time-period.

About 2,800 years ago the Pre-Dorset culture changed to a degree which makes it practical to speak of a new phase of the A.S.T. tradition called the Dorset culture. As the names of these two phases may suggest, the Dorset culture was recognized first. The name derives from the original find location of a collection of artifacts near Cape Dorset in southwestern Baffin Island. The collection was studied in 1925 by the arctic scholar, Diamond Jenness, who proposed that the Dorset culture had existed in the Arctic prior to the arrival of the Thule culture which at that time was the only generally recognized prehistoric Eskimo culture in Canada and Greenland. Today, we know that the Dorset people once occupied most of the Canadian Arctic and Greenland, and spread as far south as Newfoundland. A limited amount of skeletal material seems to indicate that the Dorset people belonged to the Inuit race, and some scientists have postulated that they also spoke an Eskimoan language. The material culture of the Dorset phase differs in some ways from Pre-Dorset. The Dorset people, for example, initially used a number of ground slate tools, and the internal arrangements and general configurations of their house structures were different. They may not have used bows and arrows or dogs and large sleds. However, in spite of these differences there can be little doubt that the Dorset culture had its roots in the preceding Pre-Dorset culture.

The Dorset culture is slightly better represented in the park area than the Pre-Dorset, and future research should yield much additional information regarding the activities of these people. We know that they hunted most of the available game species with the exception of the large baleen (bowhead) whale. That the Dorset people utilized this latter species is suggested by the location of a few sections of baleen in a stratified Dorset site near the park boundary (Figure 38).

During the later stages of their culture, the Dorset people developed a highly artistic orientation, including finely made naturalistic carvings and geometric designs which often took the form of skeletal motifs. Their winter settlements, consisting of a number of rectangular, skin-covered dwellings, were usually situated on the coast with favourable hunting conditions being the main criterion for a particular site location. The later Thule people often chose the same areas and it is most common to find Dorset artifacts mixed in with Thule culture material.

In certain areas, such as the southeastern parts of Hudson Bay, the Dorset culture lasted until about A.D. 1400 (550 BP). However, in most other areas the rigorous and uncertain conditions of human existence proved detrimental to the Dorset people. There is little reason to doubt that scattered groups of these people were still present when the Thule people entered the Canadian Arctic and Greenland from Alaska about 1,000 years ago. There are a number of old legends in the north which describe strange encounters between the Inuit and a people called the Tunit. Many of these legends probably originate from encounters between Dorset and Thule people, the former being the Tunit. Some of the present-day Inuit in Pangnirtung and Broughton can still recall many of these legends which usually portray an initially peaceful association between the two peoples. The Tunit were a taller and stronger people who would occasionally come to the aid of the Inuit in times of trouble.

> "An Inuit was once being chased by a polar bear on the ice. One of the Tunit people saw this and came to the rescue. He lifted the bear by its hind legs, swung it over his head and threw it to the ground with such a force that the bear was killed instantly. Seeing this show of strength the Inuit was almost as afraid as before and ran, leaving the bear behind for the Tunit."

From many of these stories one gets a definite impression of increasing uneasiness and mistrust between the two groups. Although the Tunit were supposedly stronger (a trait often attributed to strangers), the Inuit were usually much more intelligent. Accord-

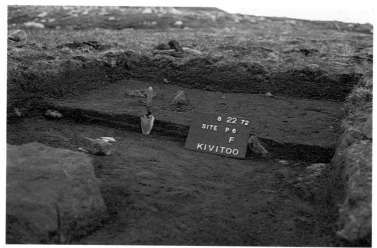

Fig. 38. Excavation unit on an A.S.T. site near the park. Frozen ground was encountered at this level, only eighteen centimetres below the surface, bringing any further progress almost to a standstill. It was in an early Dorset "level" on this site that baleen sections were found.

ing to the legends, the Tunit became more and more wary of the Inuit and eventually left the country.

Many of the old stone ruins which can be seen in and around the park area are often attributed by present-day Inuit to the Tunit. Archaeological testing of these dwellings has shown, however, that most of the structures were constructed by the Thule people.

The Thule People

The term "Thule culture" was originally used to designate a number or archaeological finds in northern Greenland by members of the Danish Second Thule Expedition. Knowledge about this culture was greatly advanced during the Fifth Thule Expedition (1921-1924), when extensive field research and excavations were carried out by the renowned arctic archaeologist Therkel Mathiassen. The leader of the expedition, Knud Rasmussen, successfully completed a great sled journey across the Canadian Arctic to Alaska with the indispensable aid of the Inuit. He noticed great similarity in both language and culture among northern Inuit communities from east to west, indicating that mobility and cultural contact were extensive.

From archaeological research in northern Alaska we know that the Thule culture originated there about 1,000 years ago (Figure 39). It was the culmination of a long period of cultural development in the Bering Strait regions since the time of the initial eastward movement of the A.S.T. people. The Thule people were well adapted to life along the arctic seas and tundra regions. With dogs, sleds, umiaks and kayaks they were very mobile and the original eastward expansion took place quite rapidly.

The climatic conditions may have been somewhat warmer than at present, with less sea ice and more favourable conditions for most sea and land mammal species. Sea mammal hunting was greatly emphasized by the Thule people, including the active and dangerous pursuit of the large baleen whale. The seasonal hunting patterns also led the Thule people in search of caribou and musk ox in regions where these animals were available.

Following the rapid eastward movement through the Arctic Islands into Greenland, the Thule people advanced into the more southerly regions. Eventually they reached the south coast of Lab-

Fig. 39. The second major migration of arctic people into the Canadian north. The present-day Inuit are direct descendants of the Thule culture Eskimos.

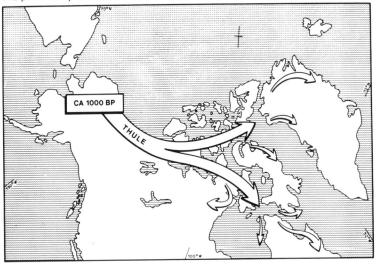

Fig. 40. Excavation units in a refuse area on a Thule winter site in Cumberland Sound. The 1.50x1.50-metre units are divided by retaining walls which can be excavated at a later time in order to check the stratigraphic sequences.

rador where any further advances were stopped by hostile Indian groups as well as white settlers. It has already been suggested that the Thule people came in contact with remnant Dorset populations, and the use of snow houses is a cultural trait which may have been picked up by the Thule people from these encounters.

The evidence from archaeological research in eastern Baffin Island suggests that the arrival of the Thule culture in the park area took place around A.D. 1200. This event is of particular interest since the present-day Inuit are direct descendants of the Thule people. Our knowledge of succeeding cultural events has been extracted through three seasons of field research and excavation. With the invaluable assistance of local inhabitants, a large number of old Thule sites were located in the vicinity of the park (mostly in Cumberland Sound). A number of these winter sites were selected for testing in order to determine which settlements had been used extensively through time, thus affording good chronological sequences. Once the sites were chosen, a number of refuse areas and dwelling structures were selected for excavation (Figure 40).

Each excavation unit was assigned a number and was then very carefully scraped or "troweled" level by level. The artifacts located

Fig. 41. Analyzing the bone refuse with the aid of Kanea Eetooangat. The bones from each level are separated according to species in order to determine any changes in the available food resources and hunting patterns through time.

between arbitrary five-centimetre levels of each unit were kept in separate containers and the precise location of each specimen was noted in the field books and unit drawings. Progress was often very slow due to the frozen ground and on one site it took four weeks to excavate only fifty centimetres in depth. All the bone refuse from each level was assembled and identified in order to investigate any possible changes in the food habits (game availability) through time (Figure 41).

House ruins were excavated in order to establish the time period of occupation and to see if several floor levels were present, indicating reuse of the same dwelling at different times. These cultural refuse deposits were most interesting in their revelations about the lives of the Thule people.

As mentioned earlier, harpoon heads are some of the best time indicators in Eskimo prehistoric research. The specimens from the lower refuse levels (Figure 42) indicated a time-period of about A.D. 1200, and subsequent radiocarbon dates from the same levels confirmed this general time-range. Radiocarbon dates are not as accurate as archaeologists would like. However, when used with caution and in conjunction with a regional comparison of the material evidence (particularly harpoon heads), reasonable time estimates can be forwarded. Massive concentrations of baleen slabs in the lower levels suggested a strong emphasis on whaling. Baleen was often used to make sleeping platform mats, drying racks, and other household features as well as drum-rims, bows and even weapon points. Ground slate was used extensively for various points, knives and the well-known woman's knife, the *ulu*. Children had a variety of toys, such as wooden dolls, stone lamps, slate *ulus* and miniature replicas of hunting equipment for boys (Figure 43). Life was their school of learning and their parents did everything they could to ensure that their children would become productive and contributing members of the community.

The Thule people did not concern themselves with artistic expression to the same extent as the Dorset people. However, an ivory comb (Figure 44) and a bow drill were decorated with a few incised scenes which helped in the reconstruction of their way of

Fig. 42. Harpoon heads, slate end blades and an arrow tip from the Thule period. The third harpoon head from the left belongs to the time period of early white contact. The two other harpoon head specimens belong to the earlier pre-contact Thule period.

0   5 cm

Fig. 43. Toy specimens from the Thule period. Toy artifacts often represent important additions to the material remains of a culture since they represent miniature copies of "life-sized" specimens. *Top right:* a soapstone lamp with a central ridge. *Bottom left to right:* a wooden doll with incised lines showing the dress pattern, a small wooden doll, a harpoon head which stylistically belongs to a late time period, a slate *ulu* (woman's knife) with a baleen grip.

life. One section of a bow drill depicted a snow house and a group of people in a large umiak (Figure 45).

Most of the very old house structures had been obliterated by the construction of more recent dwellings. From other sites we know that the early Thule winter houses were built out of sod, stone, and whalebone sections with the roof supported by whale ribs covered with skins and sod. The dwellings were usually constructed partially below ground with an entrance tunnel leading into the house slightly below the level of the central floor. The sleeping platform was raised in the rear half of the dwelling with small storage compartments situated underneath. One or two side platforms usually supported the seal-oil lamps, and the cooking and garment drying took place here. Excavation of such winter houses produced a wide range of artifacts which reflected the various activities and task distributions between men and women.

Seasonal activities were guided mostly by the changing availability of different game species. Caribou were hunted extensively in the fall when the skins were best suited for making cloth. Fishing was of prime importance during the summer months when the char were running in great numbers. In early spring, ice fishing on the lakes provided an important addition to the food supply as did the abundance of waterfowl which passed through the area during the late spring and fall. Seal hunting took place throughout the year, whether at the breathing holes on the fast-ice, along open leads, or from kayaks in the open water. Judging from the analysis of the bone refuse, the ringed seal provided a very large proportion of the food intake. The large baleen whales migrated through the area during the spring and fall and when the hunters of a settlement were fortunate enough to "catch" one of these animals, great quantities of food and fuel were assured.

People usually returned to their former winter settlements late in the fall unless there was reason to seek a new winter location. The study of one of the refuse deposits from a site in Cumberland Sound indicated that this particular winter settlement had been occupied extensively for several hundred years (Figure 46). Then,

Fig. 44. *Left to right:* an ivory comb decorated with a number of Y-designs and lines; an ivory pendant; an ivory "winged" needle case with incised line decorations; a wooden wick trimmer (for controlling the flames along the edge of the soapstone lamp) with a carved figure at the end of the handle.

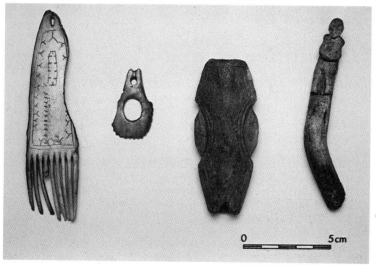

0   5cm

Fig. 45. Engraved scenes from an ivory drill bow probably illustrating a snow house with a long entrance passage, and six people in an umiak hunting a large whale.

about 300 years ago, changes took place which suggested that the inhabitants were entering upon troublesome times. At first there was an increase in the number of seals hunted, as well as a similar increase in the bone remains of other animals, such as caribou. At the same time the amount of baleen in the refuse deposits was decreasing noticeably, indicating a reduction in the number of whales caught. Whaling then came to an almost complete halt and for a short period of time the hunting of ringed seals took on tremendous proportions. Quite suddenly the site was abandoned and only used very sporadically during the following century.

What happened? We know from the paleo-climatological records that a cold climatic episode began as early as 750 years ago and that

Fig. 46. Excavation profiles of a refuse deposit. The approximate time periods are indicated and the profile suggests two major periods of occupation.

GENERAL STRATIGRAPHY

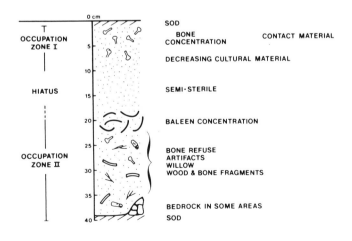

this trend really intensified about 350 years ago, ending around A.D. 1850. The last period is often referred to as "the little ice-age" at which time increasing masses of pack-ice may have forced the large whales too far away from the coast, beyond the reasonable reach of the Eskimo hunter. To compensate for this economic loss, greater emphasis was placed on ringed seal hunting. Cooling climatic conditions may initially have been beneficial to the ringed seal population, since a greater extent of fast-ice theoretically provides breeding and denning habitats for a larger number of seals. The ice cover can, however, become too thick for the younger animals who will leave the area when they are unable to keep their breathing holes open. Added hunting pressure on the ringed seal population may have further reduced their availability, and the Thule people were faced not only with the loss of the large whales but also with a decreasing ringed seal population. During this time period (350 to 100 years ago) the snow cover on land was more extensive than during the preceding 6,000 years and the overall carrying capacity of the region was sharply reduced. In order to survive this environmental shift the people had to disperse. Some groups probably headed inland in the vicinities of Amadjuak and Nettilling Lakes, where caribou hunting, fishing and some seal hunting could at least support a number of families on a year-round basis. Other groups may have chosen to live in smaller and more mobile scattered groups along the coast.

The settlement was used occasionally during the next hundred years and it was only about 200 years ago that the site was again used on a regular basis. The clearly outlined house structures dated back to this latter time period and most of them produced several floor levels indicating reoccupation on as many as three occasions. Careful excavation of the house floors showed that the inhabitants had come in contact with European and American whalers shortly after their last major reoccupation of the site. There was usually no contact material (nails, beads, clay pipe fragments) in the refuse from the bottom stone floors, but the second as well as the most recent floor level deposits showed that contact with the whalers was increasing in intensity (Figure 47). This development was to have far-reaching consequences for the Thule people.

A Time of Change

There can be little doubt that the land known as Helluland in the old Norse sagas refers to Baffin Island. Crossing Davis Strait from

Fig. 47. Artifacts of European and American affinities located in Thule winter houses from the early contact period. *From left to right, top:* Clay pipe sections with the manufacturer's inscriptions (McDougall, Glasgow). These pipes were first manufactured in the early nineteenth century; two glass beads; a lead shot. *Bottom:* A brass rim-fire cartridge; a domino piece; a brass boat nail.

Greenland, the Norsemen probably sighted the eastern coastline of the island near what is now Cape Dyer. Following the Baffin Island coast southward, they must have passed the entrance to Cumberland Sound. At present there is no archaeological evidence indicating contact between the Norse explorers and the Eskimos in this area. Future research may establish such contact; it is possible, however, that there were no native people present in southeastern Baffin Island during the first couple of centuries of Norse colonization and exploration. In any case, it is known that the Norsemen sailed past the east coast of the island from time to time. It is probably not a coincidence that the same route was used by John Davis, who, with his two ships *Sunshine* and *Moonshine*, crossed the strait which now bears his name and sighted the east coast of Cumberland Peninsula in August 1585. He discovered and named Mount Raleigh, rounded Cape Mercy on August 11, and made the first recorded entry into Cumberland Sound. From Cape Mercy he sailed sixty leagues along the north coast of the sound, and landed on an island. Considering the distance (180 nautical miles), they probably set foot on one of the many islands at the head of the sound. They had no problems with ice and only a bit of fog to contend with.

According to reports, they saw no people but there were several indications of human habitation. On August 14 and 15, they noted several stone walls and a human skull. About twenty dogs were seen, one of which wore a leather collar. They also found two sleds which reminded them of sleds made in England. One was made of fir, spruce and oaken boards sawed like "inch boards", which probably refers to ships' planking. On August 17, they noticed a structure, probably a grave, in which was found a small toy canoe and some beads with holes in one end. After naming the islands at the head of the sound the "Erle of Cumberland Islands", they departed, following the southern coastline, where they saw several signs of human habitation in the form of fire-places and house walls, probably built by the Thule people who inhabited Cumberland Sound at this time.

The presence of a sled made from fir, spruce, and particularly oaken boards suggests the presence of Europeans on the Baffin Island coast prior to John Davis. The material could have originated from Frobisher Bay, where Martin Frobisher stayed in 1576, or from the wreck of a Norse vessel, although the latter ships from Greenland used little oak and then mostly for the keel section. John Davis does mention seeing Basque whalers in the Labrador Sea and there is good reason to believe that Dutch vessels as well were plying the waters of Davis Strait at this time.

Following William Baffin's voyage in 1616 into the bay which bears his name, an increasing number of whalers began to operate in the waters between Baffin Island and Greenland. With the depletion of baleen whales in the Greenland Sea during the early part of the nineteenth century, the attention of the whalers shifted even more to the waters of Baffin Bay and Davis Strait. Although it seems unlikely that an area like Cumberland Sound was not visited from time to time by these whalers, there are no recorded entries into the sound until 1839 when Captain Penny rediscovered the large inlet, naming it "Hogarth Sound". The Penny Ice Cap and the Penny Highlands in the park have been named in honour of the captain.

The idea of establishing winter whaling stations along the coastal regions of eastern Baffin Island gained support as it became increasingly difficult to get a full catch in a single season. In 1852, American whalers established a winter station in Cumberland Sound and the British soon followed, with Captain Penny establishing a winter

Fig. 48. Whalers' graves near the old whaling station at Kekerten in Cumberland Sound. Weathering has obliterated the inscriptions on the grave markers.

station on Kekerten Island in 1853. On the north coast of the peninsula the whaling station at Kivitoo was established, now within the present park boundary. The whaling voyages took their toll in human lives and many a sailor was buried in these northern regions far away from home. The whalers' graveyards at Kivitoo and Kekerten (Figure 48) attest to the fate of some of these men, while the large number of Inuit graves from the same time period are grim reminders of the devastating effect of white intervention on the Inuit population.

The Changing Inuit Culture

The archaeological record has shown that Inuit and white contact was fairly late in the park region compared to many areas in Canada and Greenland. Once the contact was made, however, it proved to have an intense and dramatic impact on the Inuit way of life. Initially the contact provided a number of material trade items, including firearms which eventually replaced the bow and arrow, and to a lesser extent the sealing harpoon. The rifle was unfortunately useless without ammunition, and thus a dependency was established which increased with time. The skin-covered kayaks and umiaks gave way to wooden whaling boats, and wood itself became an important commodity. While the whalers needed skins for winter clothing, wool and cotton became a part of the Inuit dress. The summer tents were soon covered with canvas instead of caribou and seal skins and in time the winter structures also consisted of wood-framed, canvas-covered tents. Ground slate tools were soon replaced by metal knives and points, and the old soapstone lamps and vessels gave way to metal pots and other utensils. The metal seal-oil lamp, a close copy of the old soapstone lamp, is still used in some of the present-day hunting camps.

The increasing dependency on Western manufactured goods was only one aspect of the changes that took place. In 1840, Captain Penny estimated a population of about 1,000 Inuit in Cumberland Sound. In 1857, he brought a Moravian missionary, Warmow, to the area who estimated that the total population had decreased to about 350. In 1883, Franz Boas, the father of American anthropology, estimated a total population of about 245 in the sound. Indications are, however, that by that time a number of people had moved out of the area and settled along the north shore of Cumberland Peninsula.

The establishment of whaling stations often upset the seasonal economic cycle of the Inuit who were employed by the whalers during the spring and fall whaling. The stations were usually staffed by one to three whites plus a number of Inuit employed throughout the year. Weekly rations of coffee, molasses, tobacco and biscuits were distributed to the Inuit whose modern word for Saturday, *sivataqvik*, means "the day when biscuits are handed out".

Material and economic orientations were not the only aspects of change in the old Thule culture. Prior to white contact the Inuit populations inhabiting the coastal areas of Cumberland Sound as well as the peninsula were maintaining some form of tribal identity. The rapid population decrease upset the social structure, straining it in spite of its inherent flexibility, and the regional tribal identities of the Talirpingmiut, Qinguamiut, Kingnaitmiut, Saumingmiut, and Padlermiut, became a thing of the past. Only a few of the older Inuit can recall these divisions today.

Following the somewhat negative reports of Warmow, the Moravians decided against the establishment of a mission in the area, and the position of the *angakoq* (medicine man) was secured a little while longer. The *angakoq* was the central figure in the religious sphere of the pre-Christian Inuit culture. He, or she, communicated with the spirit world and the powerful forces which influenced the daily lives of the people. If one of the many taboos was broken, it was the *angakoq* who tried to appease the offended spirit, and in the case of illness and other misfortunes his advice was sought and carefully followed. Ceremonies and feasts were important social events for all the inhabitants of a settlement. People would gather in the *qaggi*, or "singing house", where the *angakoq* usually acted as master of ceremonies. The singer would beat his drum, often composing as he went along, while the audience listened and frequently joined in the chorus. Satirical song duels often settled arguments which might otherwise have ended quite differently for the parties concerned. Blood feuds were a threat to the whole community since one killing usually led to another. Once they were initiated, these feuds could continue for generations, thus it was of great importance for the community or tribe to dissipate the spark of open combat. Song duels and other social means of settling disputes were not always sufficient to cool the tempers, however, and families would often decide to move away from a settlement to avoid further bloodshed. A number of these old skirmishes are still recounted today, such as the story of the feud between hunters from the old settlements of Anarnitung (a small island at the head of Cumberland Sound) and Niutang (situated in the upper parts of Kingnait Fjord). One of the hunters from Anarnitung had on occasion murdered a number of hunters from Niutang, and the people from the latter settlement decided to seek revenge. They went by sled to the vicinity of the Anarnitung village and ambushed the felon as he returned to his home.

The Niutang settlement, used during times of good caribou hunting, was abandoned about A.D. 1800. Among the many house structures are the remains of a large singing house (Figures 49 and 50).

Eventually, the acculturation of the Inuit reached a point of no return. Their dependence on the worldly and not-so-wordly aspects of Western civilization was almost complete, and a decreasing number of people could have survived a complete "return to the land". The Inuit were thus placed in a precarious position, since the presence of the whites was based primarily on the uncertain availability of whales and an equally unpredictable market situation far removed from the Inuit world. At one point there was a very real possibility that the Inuit would be abandoned and forced to pick up the pieces of a half-forgotten past. Whale hunting was becoming less and less profitable. Prolonged hunting pressure had greatly reduced the bowhead population, and synthetic substitutes for baleen

Fig. 49. The large boulder-walled singing house on the Niutang site in Kingnait Fiord. The structure is more than ten metres in diameter and could house a large number of people including the *angakoq*, who occupied the area near the central rock.

together with a lessening demand for whale-oil eventually forced the closing of the whaling stations in the early part of the twentieth century. The people who had settled in the vicinity of the stations had to reestablish their former settlement patterns consisting of a number of small, semi-permanent camps. A number of these camps were situated in much the same areas as the old Thule winter sites, indicating that the geographical location of the old settlements still offered the best ecological advantages for the hunters.

As it turned out, the traders and missionaries were instrumental in warding off impending disaster, the potential for which they and the whalers had essentially created in the first place. In 1921 the Hudson's Bay Company established a trading post in Pangnirtung. A number of smaller trading outposts were maintained for a while, but their success was short-lived. The mountain behind Pangnirtung is named in memory of one of the better known traders, Duval. This man spent over fifty years in the area as a hunter, trapper and trader, and became well-known throughout Baffin Island.

Fig. 50. The large flat rock in the centre of the singing house. According to some people the many small depressions on its surface were made by the *angakoq* when he pressed his fingers down on the rock during the ceremonies.

Whaling was now mostly confined to the pursuit of white whales (beluga), and a small oil rendering station was built by the Hudson's Bay Company in Pangnirtung. Fox skins were in great demand in the Western world and provided the Inuit with an important trade commodity, at least for a while.

The first Royal Canadian Mounted Police detachment was established in Pangnirtung in 1923. Regular patrols were sent out from this centre and covered a substantial territory both north and south of Cumberland Peninsula. Births and deaths were now recorded, mail was distributed, and official Western laws were imposed on the Inuit. Prior to white contact, laws and social order had been a matter of family and peer group pressure. Regulations governing hunting and sharing, adoptions, marriages and wife-exchange, taboos and religious practices, were all incorporated in the natural learning process of each individual. The society lived by its own rules and its members were obliged to adhere to them for the common good. Leadership was a matter of recognizing the superior abilities and knowledge of a particular individual. The authority of a chief, or *issumautang* (meaning "the one who thinks"), was very limited, and there were no obligations to obey his orders. The lack of an invested central authority often led to the extended blood feuds mentioned earlier, because the inability to enforce the moral code left any kind of punitive action to the offended individual. There were some instances when "joint" community action sealed the fate of a delinquent. If a person was found to be a continuing threat to the social order of a group, he, or she, might be killed by one of the members of that group after consultation with all concerned. The victim's relatives had no moral right to revenge in such a case and the fear of social ostracism usually kept them from seeking it.

The arrival of the RCMP meant that the laws of an alien culture were forced on the Inuit. The offender now faced a court of law where if found guilty, he was ceremoniously sentenced and shipped off to jail in a foreign environment. However, law enforcement was only a small part of the activities of the RCMP whose patrols to the semi-isolated Inuit camps provided aid and relief for the less fortunate.

Fig. 51. The remains of a house structure on the recently abandoned settlement of Immigen in Cumberland Sound. The lumber was procured from the whalers and traders, and the house was originally covered with canvas. The internal arrangements of sleeping, cooking and storage areas were essentially the same as in the pre-contact dwellings.

The Anglican mission remained on Blacklead Island until 1926 when it was relocated permanently in Pangnirtung. In 1930, St. Luke's Hospital was finished and operated as the only hospital on Baffin Island in conjunction with the mission. In spite of the location of the trading post, the hospital and the mission, attempts at centralizing the Inuit population progressed very slowly. The geographical location of Pangnirtung was never advantageous to hunting. Extensive tidal flats were a hindrance to transportation, and strong winds often plagued the area. The distance to good hunting areas was great and it is no coincidence that there are very few remains of old Thule sites in Pangnirtung Fiord.

There were still sixteen camps left in Cumberland Sound in 1951 and it was not until the Canadian Federal Department of Northern Affairs became established in Pangnirtung that the Inuit began to resettle in earnest (Figure 51). Housing, schooling, social assistance and employment opportunities provided some incentive for the people to move, and the increasing use of powered modes of transportation enabled the hunters to cover greater distances in spite of the settlement location. The HBC established a post on Broughton Island in 1960, and the centralization process along the northern coast of the Peninsula advanced rapidly. Within a few years Kivitoo was abandoned, followed later by Padloping. By 1966 there were only eight camps remaining in Cumberland Sound and the Inuit population of Pangnirtung was close to 600. At present there is only one camp, located at Krepishaw on the south coast of Cumberland Sound. The camp consists of about forty people and it is probably only a matter of time before they move in to Pangnirtung.

The introduction of a cash economy broke down the cohesiveness of the Inuit community. Formerly, the camp leader would trade the skins (fox and seal) collectively from a settlement and distribute the provisions obtained equally among all. Today the skins belong to the individual hunter who can spend his money on better equipment and other items as he sees fit. This trend has not only diminished the role of the "leader" but has also created a greater disparity between the various Inuit families.

Few cultures could have endured such massive and rapid change and still retain some semblance of cultural identity. The present situation of the Inuit can only be understood in the light of events which have catapulted them from a hunting-oriented traditional culture into an often confusing modern technological culture. Nearly every aspect of their original way of life has been altered in a very short time. For many young people, boarding schools have truly widened the so-called generation gap and in some areas the Inuit language is losing ground to English. The transition is especially difficult for the younger generation who may lack any true identity with either the old ways or the new. They are often forced to make a choice between conflicting values, and live in a frightening no-man's land where parental guidance often clashes with new attitudes taught in the white man's schools. The struggle of the present-day Inuit is to assimilate these values while holding on to some vestiges of their cultural heritage.

References

Boas, Franz. *The Central Eskimo.* Lincoln: University of Nebraska Press, 1967. This work was originally published as part of the Sixth Annual Report of the Bureau of Ethnology, Smithsonian Institution, Washington, 1888.

At the age of 25 Franz Boas set out on his first scientific exploration in North America. This classic ethnographic study of the Central Eskimos is based on his field work in Cumberland Sound and the shores of the Davis Strait from 1883 to 1884. The work includes a detailed description of the tribal distributions of the Eskimos, their seasonal movements and intimate relationship to their country. The various cultural activities of the Eskimos; hunting, fishing, transportation, habitations, social and religious customs, tales and traditions etc., are described and followed by a brief but useful glossary of Eskimo words.

Harper, Kenn. *Pangnirtung.* Montreal: Harper, 1972. Available in Pangnirtung.

A discussion of events leading up to the establishment of the settlement of Pangnirtung and the subsequent developments of this community. Interesting background information on the whaling industry, early missionary activities and the trading companies.

Maxwell, Moreau S. *Archaeology in the Lake Harbour District, Baffin Island.* Ottawa: Archaeological Survey of Canada, 1973.

A detailed description of archaeological findings along the southern coast of Baffin Island, particularly in the vicinity of Lake Harbour and Frobisher Bay, this work is the most complete description to date of the cultural events of the A.S.T. occupants on Baffin Island. According to the author the Pre-Dorset people inhabited the southern regions of Baffin Island as early as 2200 B.C. establishing the base for a continuous cultural development of the A.S.T. tradition ending with the classic Dorset phase around A.D. 480.

Millward, A.E., ed. *Southern Baffin Island, An Account of Exploration, Investigation and Settlement During the Past Fifty Years.* Ottawa: Department of the Interior, 1930.

A very informative compilation of scientific expeditions and exploratory journeys in southern Baffin Island including a description of the early missionary work in Cumberland Sound, and the extensive RCMP patrols in the region. The appendix contains the fascinating story of the ill-fated exploratory attempts of Bernard A. Hantzsch in 1910. Hantzsch was the first white man to cross Baffin Island from Cumberland Sound to the east coast of Foxe Basin where he died after a prolonged illness. His written observations were returned to the sound by his Inuit companions.

3. The Living Landscape

Patrick Baird

Boreal Ecology

Ecology is a Seventies' catch-word whose meaning is little understood. To many, ecology suggests the destruction of natural beauty by man, machine and chemicals. While this is to some degree true, the deceptively simple definition of this complex science is "that branch of biology dealing with living organisms' habits, modes of life, and relations to their surroundings".

Arctic conditions affect the relationship between plants, animals and man in special ways. Since an attempt can be made to limit changes to life-systems within the boundaries of Auyuittuq National Park, it affords an excellent opportunity to observe these relationships.

Arctic life is characterized by few species but often large numbers of individuals within the species, for example, lemmings, caribou, many of the birds, willows. In general, species do not compete biologically with each other, as they do in southern regions, but are pitted against the environment. The stability of an ecological system (ecosystem) is a direct function of its complexity, hence the relatively simple arctic ecosystem with its few species and huge area is very unstable, resulting often in violent fluctuations of population in such groups as lemmings and hares, and consequently among their predators.

Unstable is a more satisfactory word to use for arctic ecosystems than *fragile*. Although arctic plant communities and animal populations are easily destroyed or altered, most of them are remarkably tough and adapted to the harsh environment in many peculiar ways, and in some cases could not survive as well elsewhere.

Adaptations of Plants

The following are examples of how plants adapt to arctic conditions:

1. *Permafrost.* Because the soil is permanently frozen often to only a few centimetres (fifty centimetres maximum) below the surface, the depths of root systems and of the burrows of animals must be limited. A further difficulty is solifluction—the creep downslope of the thawed and saturated active layer—which is a common process that can destroy vegetative cover. Permafrost does, however, preserve soil moisture by preventing deep infiltration of water despite the rather low annual precipitation in the form of rain and snow.

2. *Low winter temperature.* All parts of plants must be capable of withstanding solid freezing. One difference between the arctic and the northern forest (where winter temperatures can fall equally low) is that the roots of tundra plants, which cannot be deeper than

Fig. 52 Solifluction and slumping—permafrost melt by water.

the permafrost line, are exposed to severer cold than are the roots of forest plants and trees which are insulated by leaf litter and usually deeper snow, and are able to penetrate much further into the ground.

3. *Cool short summer.* This results in low vegetative productivity and slows the activity of pollinating insects. Plants adapt with an increase in internal temperature caused by the retention of dense mats of dead or persistent leaves. This has been found to produce a rise in temperature of as much as fifteen degrees Celsius above the surrounding air. The hanging bells of arctic heather, bear berry, and bluebell trap warm air rising from the ground. Hairy stems and woolly seed covers help, as does dark pigmentation, yet there are a surprising number of highly reflective white and yellow flowers. Some of these, such as mountain avens and arctic poppy, have parabolic-shaped flowers which turn sunward, thus concentrating heat at their centres.

The shortness of the summer season affects birds considerably, as will be described later, but for plants it almost eliminates annuals since flowering, fruiting, and seed germination must be so swift. Vegetative reproduction—the sprouting of what are, in effect, new plants from existing stems, rhizomes and root systems—is a very common means of continuing life for arctic plants. Since a severe summer can result in no new seed formation whatever, the advantages of having a secondary system of reproduction are obvious. Some plants, such as nodding saxifrage, produce small bulb clusters on their stems which eventually drop off and become new plants. As no pollination or seed formation is involved, this too is vegetative reproduction.

4. *Long day.* The twenty-four-hour daylight helps to compensate for the rigours imposed by the short summers and cold conditions. For plants to flower and set seed, energy is required beyond that needed to maintain vegetative growth. Were it not for the midnight sun the Arctic would support far fewer species than it does, simply because the necessary energy to fuel the ecosystem would not be available. An interesting feature of many arctic plants is that they demand twenty-four-hour daylight throughout their reproductive period and do not flourish when transplanted to the south, even though conditions for growth would seem to be more favourable.

5. *Low nitrogen supply.* Due to slow bacterial activity there tends to be a shortage of nitrogen in the arctic soil. Some species, however, seem well adapted to this too and are unable to take in in-

creased nitrogen. On the other hand, many grasses and some other plants react favourably to the manuring below bird cliffs, on owl perching spots, old camp sites, and fox "watering posts".

6. *Strong wind.* This is the greatest hazard to all life in the north. In winter its effect is cumulative since it smooths the land roughness by filling the hollows with drift snow, thus impeding the normal reduction of wind speed near the ground by eddying. Wind affects plants by flailing (if stems are long), by dessication, and particularly by sand and snow abrasion. Cold winter snow composed of hard small crystals is as damaging as sand grains. So early, warmer, hence softer, snowfall is important to preserve plants, which in the main, however, take refuge by forming low dense mats with no living parts left above the snow surface. Arctic heather, for example, flourishes in lee positions where early snow cover forms, and attenuates rapidly where winter exposure occurs. One good effect of the wind, however, is its distribution of seed over a wide area.

Adaptations of Mammals and Birds

Mammals and birds also have adaptations to the environment which in some ways are advantageous to their activities, in others detrimental. Some, of course, including most birds, migrate south in winter; most mammals either undergo a limited form of hibernation (such as the female polar bear), store food and contrive shelter (such as the lemming), or have enormously improved insulation compared to their southern relatives.

Northern birds and mammals tend to have a long physiological build-up which allows them to bear their young, and raise them, in suitable locations and at convenient times of the year. Migrant bird species arrive at Baffin's summering ground on almost the same date every year. Having estimated their tolerance to the frequent early-summer cold spells, and having worked their way north feeding hard, they are generally fat and in good condition. On arrival they often find no new vegetation growth and few live insects, but the rapid quick-freeze of lichens, grasses, and berries during the preceding fall will have preserved their nutritive value, and the females, at least, fare well on these and on the larvae of insects. The males are often heavily engaged in securing "territory" and depend to a greater extent on their fat storage.

By the time the young have hatched, however, new green growth is abundant and insects are plentiful. The snow bunting (almost invariably the first migrant to arrive) delays its breeding to coincide with that of later-comers so that this lavish food supply will be available when its nestlings are most demanding. But the season is short, and compared to the same species further south, there appear to be no differences here in terms of number of eggs laid, time of incubation, and time until the young are fully fledged. The short season also means that replacing a destroyed clutch of eggs is difficult, and raising two broods almost impossible, even during extremely favourable summers.

In an environment in which low temperatures and strong winds are major factors, any adaptation or characteristic which aids an animal to maintain essential warmth is favoured. The first obvious characteristic is the insulation provided by heavy fur. For those few birds that are year-round residents, insulation is provided by feathers which in the case of the ptarmigan and snowy owl extend to the toes. Thick layers of blubber permit the marine mammals to live in the icy arctic waters. The shorter ears of such mammals as the arctic fox and the arctic hare as compared with their southern cousins are another adaptation to reduce heat loss. Arctic animals are quite often much larger than their southern relatives. This might not appear to be an advantage, but the larger size means that there is proportionately less surface area per unit of body volume over which heat loss can occur.

The insulation of large arctic mammals is so great that they can maintain essential warmth without increased metabolic rate. The arctic fox (together with the white dall sheep of the Yukon Mountains) has such a splendid winter coat that it needs to increase heat production by activity only at around forty degrees below zero. In contrast, certain tropical animals need a three-fold metabolic increase to maintain essential warmth when the temperature drops to just ten degrees Celsius.

The ermine and lemming are much less well provided for, and protect themselves from winter cold by staying much of the time beneath the insulating snow cover. The lemming makes nests of hay which furnish food as well as shelter, and the ermine pursues it in its snowy hideouts.

Many of the marine mammals migrate, in this case not to seek warmer climates, but to avoid being trapped beneath winter ice, which sometimes happens with distressing consequences to white whales and narwhal. Walrus may over-winter in regions where strong currents and tides prevent ice formation, but the water must be shallow enough to allow them to dive (up to a hundred metres) for the clams which are their principal diet.

The ring and bearded seals have the ability to maintain open breathing holes. The former, like the harp seal which breeds on the pack ice off Labrador and in the Gulf of St. Lawrence, bears a white-coat pup. This splendidly warm fur lasts long enough for the baby to stay warm (when dry) through the nursing period during which it puts on blubber from the incredibly fat-rich mother's milk (50 per cent). Protected by this layer of fat, it can then safely make the transition to the marine environment. The bearded seal pup is endowed with good insulation, but grows and develops blubber even faster and is soon in the water.

Ecosystems Within the Park

As the glaciers withdrew from much of the ground that is now ice-free within the park boundaries, the plant and animal communities began to recolonize from without or perhaps from occasional unglaciated hilltops and coastal margins.

Developing slowly or rapidly depending on the kind of soil available (varying from bare rock to fine sand), a number of plant communities have become established. Many of them that we see today will probably develop no further; others are still evolving to more continuous plant cover. Because there is such a wide variety of physical factors operating to control the arctic ecosystem there is a corresponding variety of communities. One way of describing them is as follows:

1. *Fell field communities.* Here the vegetation is open. It is so scantily developed that the ground is never covered with a complete sward but individual plants are scattered over its surface. We can distinguish:

   (a) The rock desert community with crustaceous and foliose lichens (rock tripe) growing on the rocks, and between them other lichens, mosses and cushion plants, such as moss campion (*Silene acaulis*) and various saxifrages. One of the hardiest plants of all, often the first to colonize a glacier's moraine, is the yellow arctic poppy (*Papaver radicatum*).

   (b) Gravel flat communities. On the frequently flooded areas of braided streams, often covered by persistent icing (*aufeis*), the short growing season again restricts vegetation to the hardiest of the colonizers.

Fig. 53. Rock desert.

Fig. 54. Gravel flat community.

2. *Tundra communities.* Here the vegetation is more continuous, the winter's snow protection more complete. Distinguishable are:

(a) Dwarf shrub—heath tundra. The creeping willows, dwarf birch and berry-bearing members of the heath family are interspersed with arctic heather (*Cassiope*) and a carpet of mosses and "moss" lichens (*Cladonia*). This is the most diverse of the plant communities and the most colourful area of the tundra.

(b) The grassland tundra. On the damper and rawer soils and on alluvial flats of former rivers and lakes, grasses and sedges predominate with, in the wetter parts, great development of sphagnum moss and cotton grass (*Eriophorum*). Where differential frost heaving in wet soil is dominant typical tussocks (*Thufur* in Iceland) develop. Each tussock, which can be a foot or more in height, has a core of heaved mineral soil and a tuft of dead rhizomes and leafbases on the top and sides. It can afford one of the more abominable walking surfaces in the tundra area.

3. *Shore communities.* There is a normal development of salt-tolerant grasses and sedges in tidal flats in the Arctic together with the sandwort (*Arenaria*), scurvy grass (*Cochlearia*) and the sea pink.

Fig. 55. Dwarf shrub heath community.

Fig. 56. Grassland tundra.

4. *Snow patch communities.* Snowbeds which last into late summer have their own specialized vegetation. Here *Saxifraga oppositifolia* will flower late, and *Saxifraga cernua* and *Saxifraga nivalis* prefer these moist sites.

In the park all of these communites will be found, but scattered in a way that defies easy description of locations for each. Vegetation can be found as high as 1,300 metres above sea level on protected southern slopes in Pangnirtung Pass, but on the northern side of the Penny Ice Cap seldom exceeds half this altitude.

At both ends of Pangnirtung Pass a comparatively rich flora flourishes. The entire range can be seen, from lusher vegetation on the valley floor to the pioneering plants on the most recent side moraines. North of Windy Lake, however, there is a sharp reduction in species, whereas in Owl Valley the richer flora persists as far up as Highway Glacier's moraine. In this half of the pass grasses and sedges are dominant on the valley floor, and large areas of *Thufur* up to half a metre in height occur. Owl Valley at one time must have supported a considerable number of caribou judging from the number of discarded antlers found there.

Once a viable vegetation cover is established the herbivores can

Fig. 57. Differential frost-heave tussocks.

Fig. 58. Snowpatch community.

Fig. 59. Owl Valley grass sedge community with *Thufur.*

move in, and the most important link in the food chain on which most predators depend—the lemming—can establish itself. This little animal has enormous population fluctuations, still not completely understood. It tends to rise to peak numbers every four years or so and then crashes to a very low density. The lemming and other mammals are discussed later in this chapter.

Micro-habitats

The abundance of micro-habitats is one of the most striking indications of the region's harsh environment. Every advantage, no matter how slight, afforded by favourable exposure, better soil, slightly warmer microclimate, is exploited. An astonishing variety of basically different plant communities can be encountered during a very short walk. This is particularly noticeable when one is traversing the well-vegetated lateral moraines of Pangnirtung Pass.

Disturbances to the Ecosystem

The establishment of a national park in this area has meant that some of the environmental threats that cause concern in other parts of the Canadian north have been avoided. There is no danger of chemical pollution from mine, mill and smelter operations, for example, though radioactive fallout—which affected the lichen-caribou-human food chain in a large swathe of the northland after atmospheric nuclear tests were carried out—is still a hazard.

Roads and pollution from automobiles and their often unthinking passengers are no problem here. We must ensure, however, that pedestrian traffic does not create too much disturbance to the environment, such as might occur from continual use of a single defined path. It seems likely that if the rules given in Chapter 4 are properly followed, the park visitor will for many years be able to study and enjoy tundra life at close quarters as well as the spectacular scenery which surrounds it.

Flowering Plants

Visitors to Baffin Island are often surprised by its wealth of flowering plants. Botanically speaking, the land is poor in numbers of species and in annual vegetative production, but considering the long, very cold winter and brief summer, it is gratifying that there is so much to admire.

As with nesting birds, there is a rush to complete the biological process as soon as spring arrives. Flowering and seed formation is very rapid, and in poor summers may fail. Although air temperatures indicate a very short period when growth is possible, the local climate *within* the plant itself, or as a result of its sheltering neighbours, may be much more favourable. South-facing slopes, snow cover, and above all, protection from dessicating and sand-bearing wind have great effects on success.

In most of the park, only a high altitude community of plants can be found and the vegetation limit is reached at about 1,100 metres. The flora is certainly richer in the lower ground around Pangnirtung, in the Kingnait Valley, the south-facing slopes of Maktak Fiord and some areas to the southwest of the Penny Ice Cap, but even here the species count is lower than, for example, at Frobisher Bay.

Ground cover may be near complete or very open. In the former case lower and damper ground may be grass-, sedge-, and moss-covered; higher up, the drier slopes will often have a cover of dwarf shrubs. The dwarf shrubs belong to the willow, birch, and heath families. They all have woody stems, but with the exception of the occasional willow in a very favourable spot, these creep along the ground instead of being upstanding. All are thus a source of fuel, and all provide food for mammals and some birds; caribou and hares browse on the twigs and buds of the willow, ptarmigan eat the crowberries.

The descriptions and illustrations that follow should aid in the identification of most of the common plants. This is by no means an exhaustive treatment of the flora of Auyuittuq National Park and readers who wish to pursue the subject further should consult the reference given at the end of this section (p. 136).

Where common names exist, they have been supplied; where they do not, the international Latin names are used.

SALICACEAE—WILLOW FAMILY

Salix L.

Willows are the bushiest and most widespread of the plants in our area, occurring wherever there is sufficient moisture. On favoured sunny slopes they may grow to a metre in height, but mostly the branches creep closely along the ground.

Several species of willow are present, but even the experts find differentiation difficult. Some of them are *large willows* with lance-shaped leaves and upstanding catkins which become tufts of down. These may be *S. arctica*, *S. cordifolia* or *S. arctophila*. Two tiny willows with dark green leathery leaves may be distinguished from their larger brethren above. *S. herbacea* and *S. reticulata* with racket-shaped leaves, the latter with a very distinct network of veins, occupy ground which is late snow covered.

All willows are fodder for birds and mammals; twigs, bark, buds, and leaves are favoured by caribou, hares, lemmings, and ptarmigan. The dry dead branches of the larger species are a useful emergency fuel—but please use only the truly dead pieces.

BETULACEAE—BIRCH FAMILY

Betula L.

The dwarf birch is rare on Cumberland Peninsula, but one of the species, *B. nana*, has here its only locality in North America, whereas it is common in Greenland and arctic Eurasia.

Both this species and the more widespread *B. glandulosa* have typical birch leaves, nearly round, dark green paddles with crenellated edges. *B. glandulosa* has resin-filled warts on the smooth brown twigs; *B. nana* somewhat hairy twigs without warts.

Birches have been found in Kingnait Pass and to the southwest of the park. But they must be present within the park boundaries, though it will take a very keen-eyed observer to locate them.

Willow *Salix* sp.

POLYGONACEAE—BUCKWHEAT FAMILY

Mountain sorrel   *Oxyria digyna* (L.) Hill

Along damp or running watercourses you will find the arctic salad. A cluster of green or bronze, kidney-shaped leaves on separate stalks is crowned with a single stem ten to twenty centimetres bearing at the top a bunch of small disc-shaped red flowers. The leaves are excellent eating and form a good source of vitamin C. It is common in the park valleys.

Knotweed (Bistort) *Polygonum viviparum* L.

One or two stems, up to fifteen centimetres high, are crowned with a toothbrush-like spike of white or pale pink tiny flowers. Lower down are bulbils which are the main reproductive elements of the herb. Leaves are lance-like with a prominent median line up to five centimetres long, dark green and shiny. A small twisted root is edible, preferably when cooked. Common in tundra meadows, especially when well-manured.

Mountain sorrel
Oxyria digyna

Knotweed (Bistort)
Polygonum viviparum

CARYOPHYLLACEAE—PINK FAMILY

Starwort   *Stellaria longipes* Goldie (s. lat.)

A common flower in most types of habitat. It is star-shaped with five deeply divided white petals, so deeply that it appears to have ten, and short stems (five centimetres or so) bearing pairs of linear blue-green leaves.

Mouse-ear chickweed   *Cerastium alpinum L.*

Distinguished from the above by larger, less open, less deeply divided flowers and by "mouse ear"-shaped leaves cupping the stem. Stem and leaves are very hairy. Prefers drier, sandy habitats. Much rarer and in moist localities is *C. cerastoides* with deeper-notched petals and several short stalks from a creeping stem system.

Starwort   *Stellaria longipes*

Mouse-ear chickweed
Cerastium alpinum

CARYOPHYLLACEAE—PINK FAMILY *(Cont.)*

Sandwort   *Arenaria peploides* L.

On sand dunes and beaches you will find this sprawling plant with many branching fleshy stems, at each branch a pair of *elliptical* leaves and often a tiny white flower. The whole plant, when fresh, is edible.

Moss campion   *Silene acaulis* L.

This little cushion plant, studded with pink flowers, is common throughout the area and will be familiar to all alpinists, since it occurs in alpine regions throughout the northern hemisphere.

Sandwort *Arenaria peploides*

Moss campion *Silene acaulis*

CARYOPHYLLACEAE—PINK FAMILY *(Cont.)*

Bladder campion   *Melandrium affine* (J. Vahl) Hartm.

The obvious bladder (football)-shaped calyx with purple stripes is the key to this plant. Pairs of thin lance-like leaves are on the stem, from which sprout at the top one to three bladders with white or pale pink flowers with five petals.

Two rarer species are also recorded in the park: *M. apetalum* with a fatter, usually nodding bladder from which the petals scarcely appear; *M. triflorum* has three flowers and bladders at the *summit* of the stalk, not on separate short stalks as with *M. affine*. *M. triflorum* is at the southernmost end of its range in Canada. It is common in Greenland.

RANUNCULACEAE—CROWFOOT FAMILY

Buttercups   *Ranunculus* L.

There are perhaps five species of these yellow flowered plants growing in the region. They prefer moist spots, often at the edge of late snow beds.

Commonest is *R. nivalis*, or snow buttercup, with stems five to ten centimetres high, bearing glove-shaped leaves, and a five-petalled flower, smooth underneath. Very similar is *R. sulphureus* but it has a growth of brownish hairs below the flower cup. *R. lapponicus*, or Lapland buttercup, has six or more paler yellow petals on a bare long stem; the separate leaves are deeply tri-lobed.

Two crawling buttercups are *R. pygmaeus*, or dwarf buttercup, and *R. hyperboreus*, the former very small, the latter often growing in water.

PAPAVERACEAE—POPPY FAMILY

Arctic poppy   *Papaver radicatum* Rottb.

Even in the most barren areas, the tall hairy stems and large yellow (sometimes white) four-petalled flowers will be seen. The hairy, heart-shaped leaves form a dense clump. Nodding buds resemble southern poppy species.

Bladder campion
Melandrium affine

Buttercup
Ranunculus sp.

Arctic poppy
Papaver radicatum

CRUCIFERAE—MUSTARD FAMILY

Scurvy grass   *Cochlearia officinalis* L.

A shore plant which is common only where bird manuring is comparatively heavy. Many branched *spade-shaped* leaves and *rosettes* of tiny white flowers distinguish it from sandwort, which often favours the same localities. As a source of vitamin C it is good, but the scurvy-ridden park visitor would do better to look for sorrel.

Whitlow-grass   *Draba* L.

These rather undistinguished small plants with their seldom-used English name may interest the very keen only. *D. lactea* and *D. glabella* have been found in the park. Their small *four*-petalled white flowers crown slim stalks which spring from a mat of oblong leaves. In the former case, the stems are bare; in *D. glabella*, they bear a few toothed leaves.

SAXIFRAGACEAE—SAXIFRAGE FAMILY

Nodding saxifrage   *Saxifraga cernua* L.

A single stem with five-petalled white flower, large (more than one centimetre diameter) when mature, drooping when young. Basal leaves on slender stalks have a very recognizable three- or five-lobed kidney shape. Higher up on the fifteen-centimetre stem, leaves are small with fewer lobes and have small red bulb clusters which in fact fall off and become new plants. Grows on moist gravelly ledges; moderately common in our area.

Purple saxifrage   *Saxifraga oppositifolia* L.

Low matted or creeping leaves in groups of four crowned with small, very short stalked, five-petalled purple flowers, five millimetres in diameter. Grows in moist gravelly spots as high up the mountains as any flower, is often the first flower of spring, and may be hard to find in flower in July, except in shady places.

Whitlow grass *Draba* sp.

Nodding saxifrage
Saxifraga cernua

SAXIFRAGACEAE—SAXIFRAGE FAMILY *(Cont.)*

Prickly saxifrage   *Saxifraga tricuspidata* Rottb.

From a matted cushion of densely crowded yellow, green or red-brown leaves *with distinct prongs* rise ten- to fifteen-centimetre stalks crowned with five-petalled creamy white flowers, often with tiny orange spots. Very small alternate leaves grow on the stalk. It is common in all dry localities, often in good-sized clumps and is rather late flowering.

Other saxifrage species are less common. They include *S. caespitosa*, which is very hard to allot to certain supposed subspecies and will be neglected here.

S. foliosa and *S. nivalis* both have five- to twenty-centimetre stalks growing from a basal rosette of "saxifrage" type leaves—paddle-shaped with toothed ends. The flowers of *S. foliosa* are often replaced by bulb clusters on several branches from the main stems; those of *S. nivalis* are in a single cluster at the stem head and have large purple sepals. *S. foliosa* prefers moist spots whereas *S. nivalis* will be found on dry or stony places.

S. rivularis is a dwarf species which likes wet slopes below well-manured bird cliffs. It has many glove-shaped leaves on separate stalks, small white flowers, the petals three to five millimetres long, the sepals only half this.

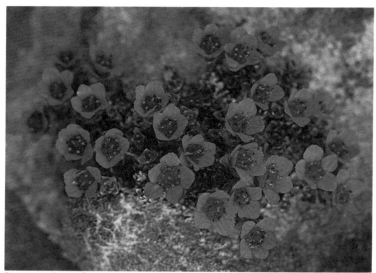

Purple saxifrage *Saxifraga oppositifolia*

Prickly saxifrage *Saxifraga tricuspidata*

ROSACEAE—ROSE FAMILY

Cinquefoil   *Potentilla* L.

The potentillas are a difficult genus to differentiate, but they are in evidence all over the park tundra with their bright yellow flowers with five overlapping petals and strawberry-like leaves. *P. nivea* and *P. hyparctica* are species with taller stems; *P. vahliana*, a shorter-stemmed species with a very dense mat of leaves, is rarer, since it favours localities rich in lime.

Mountain avens   *Dryas integrifolia* M. Vahl

The official flower of the Northwest Territories is abundant in every type of habitat. The eight-petalled, sun-following, large white flower springs from a short stalk at the base of which is a mat of flat, crenellated leaves. You will often see earlier-flowering stems bearing only the seed capsules growing beside flower-bearing stems.

Cinquefoil *Potentilla* sp.

Mountain avens *Dryas integrifolia*

EMPETRACEAE—CROWBERRY FAMILY

Crowberry   *Empetrum nigrum* L.

A creeping dwarf shrub, many branched with linear spiky leaves of bright green colour, three to four millimetres long. Tiny crimson flowers can be seen in early spring, but soon the black shiny berries form. They are not so palatable to the human, but the ptarmigan love them.

ONAGRACEAE—EVENING PRIMROSE FAMILY

Broad-leaved willow-herb   *Epilobium latifolium* L.

Perhaps the showiest of the park's flora, this arctic cousin of the fireweed has four large pink-purple petals separated by a cross of deeper purple sepals. The flowers are borne on a reddish stem with alternate dark green, fleshy, lance-shaped leaves. It grows, often in spectacular clumps, up to thirty centimetres in height along river banks and other floodable soils. Leaves and flowers are occasionally eaten by the Inuit as salad.

Crowberry *Empetrum nigrum*

Broad-leaved willow-herb *Epilobium latifolium*

PYROLACEAE—WINTERGREEN FAMILY

Large-flowered wintergreen   *Pyrola grandiflora* Rad.

This beautiful flower is well represented, particularly on southern slopes. From nearly round, dark-green, leathery basal leaves comes a strong straight stalk ten to twenty centimetres high bearing on its upper third alternate, drooping, white or pale pink flowers.

ERICACEAE—HEATH FAMILY

Labrador tea   *Ledum decumbens* (A.T.) Lodd

This familiar sweet-scented shrub grows on moderately dry tundra. The many branches are crowned with thin, straight, dark green leaves and a tuft of white flowers. It is here at about its northern limit in Canada. Further south, it is well known for making campers' mattresses. A spoonful of its leaves will make a cup of acceptable "tea".

Azalea   *Loiseleuria procumbens* (L.) Desv.

The creeping, many-branched arctic member of this group has azalea-like, elliptical median-lined leaves, topped with clusters of very small pink flowers. It is very rare in this region, again at its northern limit.

Large-flowered wintergreen *Pyrola grandiflora*

Labrador tea *Ledum decumbens*

ERICACEAE—HEATH FAMILY *(Cont.)*

Arctic heather   *Cassiope tetragona* (L.) D. Don

This common heath forms a widespread ground cover on moderately dry tundra. The tiny dark green leaves sheathe the stem in groups of four. The flower is white, bell-shaped and drooping. Cassiope grows in dense clumps, the older dying stems turning brown, which because of their resin content, burn well when dry.

Much rarer are two other heaths: *Cassiope hypnoides* resembling a moss with very small white bell flowers *with red calyxes* which grows on late snow bed areas, where also may be found *Phyllodoce coerulea* with purple closed bell flowers and flat needle-like leaves on the stalk.

Lapland rhododendron   *Rhododendron lapponicum* (L.) Wahlenb.

A branching shrub somewhat similar to the azalea with similarly shaped leaves, but with rusty undersides and woodier stems. The flower is purplish and is a miniature true rhododendron, five-petalled, one or two centimetres broad, with long, curved stamens. It is present in Weasel Valley below Tirokwa Mountain, and in other dry lowland areas.

Arctic heather *Cassiope tetragona*

Lapland rhododendron *Rhododendron lapponicum*

ERICACEAE—HEATH FAMILY *(Cont.)*

Bearberry   *Arctostaphylos alpina* (L.) Spreng.

Another rarity here. Dark green *net veined* leaves and dull red berries turning black when ripe distinguish it from cranberry. The berries are mealy with large seeds, and not recommended.

Bilberry   *Vaccinium uliginosum* L.

A common ground cover on the tundra. It has slim woody stems with clusters of nearly round, heavily-veined, small leaves, four to five millimetres in diameter, and tiny two-millimetre, bulb-shaped pink flowers. The purple berries, of course, make good eating for birds, humans and even the polar bear, which will wander inland in the fall looking for them.

Cranberry   *Vaccinium Vitis-idaea* L.

Much rarer in this area, this shrub may be found in the lowest, most favourable localities. The dark green *smooth* shiny leaves and dark red shiny berries are distinctive—the leaves oval, median lined, and the fruit delicious.

DIAPENSIACEAE—DIAPENSIA FAMILY

Diapensia lapponica (L.)

A tiny dwarf shrub found on ledges or gravel. From a four- to five-centimetre hemispherical tuft of tiny curved yellow-green leaves, neat, small, five-petalled white flowers protrude on short stalks.

Bilberry *Vaccinium uligonosum*

Diapensia lapponica

PLUMBAGINACEAE—LEADWORT FAMILY

Thrift   *Armeria maritima* (Mill.) Willd.

On gravelly flood plains and beaches, this easily-recognizable tufty plant can be found. The leaves are long and stringy; the thin, crooked, tall stems are crowned with a rosette of pink flowerettes.

SCROPHULARIACEAE—FIGWORT FAMILY

Lousewort   *Pedicularis* (L.)

This genus is widespread and readily recognizable. But the species differentiation is complicated and a job for the professional botanist.

Broadly speaking, the yellow variety will be *P. flammea*, the pink-purple either *P. hirsuta* (hairy lousewort) or *P. lanata* (woolly lousewort).

Lousewort springs from a yellowish root which is like a miniature parsnip and is edible. The leaves are alternate and fern-like and the woolly stalk is crowned with a dense group of helmet-like flowers. Height is around ten to fifteen centimetres.

Thrift *Armeria maritima*

Lousewort
Pedicularis sp.

CAMPANULACEAE—BLUEBELL FAMILY

Harebells   *Campanula uniflora* L. and *C. rotundifolia* L.

Our only blue flowers, but the colour invariably fades if picked. Both species are present. *C. uniflora* has an always solitary small flower less than one centimetre in diameter; *C. rotundiflora* is larger (more than one centimetre) with sometimes more than one flower on the stem, and stems are often more numerous and taller.

COMPOSITAE—SUNFLOWER FAMILY

Fleabane   *Erigeron eriocephalus* J. Vahl

Long, thin, shaggy leaves, a stout shaggy stem and a tufted composite flower with lilac rays and light brown centre. Five to fifteen centimetres in height, but rather uncommon in the park since it is a lime lover, and hence occurs mostly on glacial till.

Everlasting   *Antennaria* Gaertn.

Two species are to be found here. Subspecies of *A. angustata* have single flower tufts or at most a second. *A. Ekmaniana* has a bunch of three to five tufts, greyish-white in colour.

Sunflower   *Arnica alpina* (L.) Olin.

Perhaps the largest "flower" we can see. Its yellow disc is similar to our well-known sunflowers; a stout stem up to twenty or thirty centimetres carries one or two pairs of leaves, thin and long.

Dandelion   *Taraxacum lapponicum* Kihlm

No mistaking the arctic dandelion with the long, fleshy, edible deeply-incised leaves and dark yellow flower several centimetres wide. A narrower leafed species, *T. lacerum*, is reported from Maktak Fiord.

Harebell
Campanula uniflora

Dandelion
Taraxacum sp.

Sunflower
Arnica alpina

We cannot omit descriptions of some forms of vegetation other than the showy flowering plants. A large portion of the tundra biomass is made up of lichens, mosses, grasses, and rushes. Even a few mushrooms occur, none of which are deadly, but over-indulgence in them has been known to cause stomach upsets.

Of the lichens, you can identify "Tripe de roche" or rock tripe sprouting from the rocks, or *Rhizocarpon geographicum*, from which chronological dating can be established. Various forms of "reindeer moss" (*Cladonia sp.*) and the orange splash of *Caloplaca elegans* where rock faces have been manured, are identifiable.

Mossy stream banks abound, and here and on tundra meadows *Lycopodium selago* (clubmoss) is frequent. In these watery spots the delicate little fern (*Woodsia*) flourishes, and in swampy meadows horsetail (*Equisetum*) and cotton grass appear. The latter provides two species, *Eriophorum angustifolium* with three cotton heads, and *E. Scheuchzeri* with one.

Reference

The best treatment of arctic flora is found in A.E. Porsild, *Illustrated Flora of the Canadian Arctic Archipelago*, Bulletin no. 146, Biological Series no. 50 (Ottawa: Department of Northern Affairs and Natural Resources, 1957); reprinted by the National Museum of Natural Sciences, National Museums of Canada, 1973. This manual is available through Information Canada bookstores or by mail directly from: National Museums of Canada, Marketing Services Division, Ottawa, Ontario K1A 0M8.

Horsetail
Equisetum

Cotton grass
Eriophorum sp.

The Birds

One of the greatest charms of the arctic spring and summer is the proliferation of nesting and breeding birds. There are many individuals but rather few species, making bird identification quite simple, even for the inexperienced bird-watcher. A further advantage is the twenty-four hours of daylight in which to observe the frantic avian activity. There are no frustratingly obscure warblers here hiding behind a leafy screen. The sweep of tundra view, and a good amount of patience, will enable the park visitors to identify almost all the birds.

The great western plain and lakes of Baffin Island are excellent breeding areas for many kinds of geese, ducks and shorebirds, some of which spill over on migration or by accident to the eastern mountain area. Migrants from Bylot Island—nesting area of a few special species—may also pass through the park or be seen in its neighbouring waters.

Very few birds overwinter in the park area. With the exception of the little dovekie in any open waters, and the ptarmigan, raven and snowy owl on land, most others are migrants, and when the snow bunting returns from southern fields at the beginning of May, spring has begun. The next six weeks or so are the busiest—territories are established and eggs laid, often in nests of previous years to save precious time. Incubation must begin with the first egg laid because spring temperatures are still so low. This often results in broods at varied stages of development, most noticeably in snowy owl families. By the end of July most young are fledged, and many species begin to flock and start travelling toward their winter homes.

Breeding success depends enormously on the summer weather. In good seasons some birds raise large broods; but a cold and wet season may destroy either eggs or young. A good many non-breeders summer in the north as well.

The descriptions and illustrations which follow will help in the identification of most of the birds likely to be seen in Auyuittuq National Park.

LOONS

Red-throated loon   *Gavia stellata*   Koksaut (L. 61 to 68.6 cm.)
Common loon   *Gavia immer*   Koksaut (L. 71.1 to 88.9 cm.)
Arctic loon   *Gavia arctica*   Koksaut (L. 58.4 to 73.6 cm.)

Three kinds of loon *may* be seen or heard in the park, but the commonest and only certain breeder is the *red-throated loon.* These large "divers" are readily distinguished from ducks by their posture on the water: body lower, head often upstretched, and longer neck (shorter, though, than those of geese) carried lower than the back in flight. The rufous-red throat patch and the white stripes extending up the back of the grey head are unmistakable field marks. With their legs attached far back on the body they are crippled shufflers on land and hence nest close to the shore of ponds and small lakes. As a result, their eggs (two, olive or dark brown with splotches of blackish brown) are often washed away by suddenly rising water.

They usually feed in the sea and their mournful cackling will be heard in flight to and from the nest area. Their fare is small fish which are not often available in their inland habitat.

The other two loons breed on Baffin's west wetlands. The *common loon* is larger. Note its "necklace", banded back, and straight thick bill compared to the slight upturn of the red-throated's. Even rarer is the *arctic loon* with *black* throat and pearly-grey neck and head.

Common loon
Red-throated loon
Arctic loon

TUBENOSES

Northern fulmar   *Fulmarus glacialis*   Kakhodlik (L. 45.7 to 50.8 cm.)

Cape Searle, adjacent to the park, is one of the few large breeding stations of the northern fulmar in Canada. More than 100,000 of these gull-like birds nest here, then spend the other ten months of the year ranging to mid-Atlantic. Their aeroplane-like flight—rapid stiff-winged beats followed by wave high glides—is most distinctive. Colour phases vary from light to medium sooty-grey, and in the pale grey phase fulmars may be distinguished from gulls by the heavier neck and head, shorter tail, and at close range by the stubby yellow bill with its peculiar tubular nostrils. You will see them in the outer reaches of all the fiords, particularly in the northern section of the park. A single egg is laid on a cliff ledge or plateau during the first half of June and hatches in early August. (See illustration p. 169.)

SWANS

Whistling Swan   *Olor columbianus*   Kujjuk (L.121.9 to 139.7 cm., wingspan 215.9 cm.)

The whistling swan is the common wild swan of the eastern arctic. Migrating in long wavering lines or loose V-shaped flocks, the adult's huge *pure-white* wings, long slender neck and *black* bill distinguish it from the smaller, chunkier snow goose with its black-tipped wings and short neck. Adult plumage is pure white, somewhat rust-stained about the head and neck. Immature swans are a pale grey-brown, and their bills are pinkish with a black or dusky tip. The voice is a loud musical cooing note, somewhat similar to, but softer than, the honking of the Canada goose.

It is just possible that a visitor to the park may see this huge bird

Whistling swan

on migration, though it is not thought to breed in the park. The whistling swan nests on Baffin's western lowlands. Watson saw seven swans flying south through Pangnirtung Pass one July 31, and seven swans were again sighted from a mountaintop in the summer of 1974, flying down Kingnait Fiord at an altitude of approximately 2,700 metres. Besides eating them, the Inuit have made various uses of swans. The fine down has served as a "seal detector" when hung over a seal-hole as it moves when a seal surfaces. The skin of the webbed feet has been made into pouches for tobacco and other items.

Swans fly with long necks outstretched, forming a very recognizable silhouette. They seem to mate for life.

GEESE

Canada goose *Branta canadensis*   Nerdlerk (L.55.9 to 101.6 cm.)
Brant *Branta bernicla* Nerdlanak (L. 58.4 to 76.2 cm.)
Snow goose *Anser caerulescens* Kanguk (L.63.5 to 76.2 cm.)

Probably the Canada goose, or "honker", is the only breeding species in the park, particularly in the northern sections such as Maktak Fiord. But the snow goose and brant might be seen, the former on migration from further north, the latter occasionally spilling over from Baffin west. Sexes look alike at all seasons. Geese moult their flight feathers in late summer and are sometimes captured at this season by native northerners who drive them into corrals.

The *Canada goose* is found here at the end of its range. Well-known and easily identified by its black head and neck and large white cheek-patch, it nests on the margins of streams with usually four to six, but sometimes up to ten white eggs in a clutch. Goose

Canada goose
Brant

droppings (cigarillo size) and tracks will often be seen on mudflats even if no birds are around.

The *brant* is a small goose with a black head, neck and breast and only a small white patch on the sides of the neck which does not extend to the cheek as does that of the "honker". On the water its tail rides much higher than that of the Canada goose.

Few will fail to differentiate between the "honkers" and the *snow goose* which is almost pure white with black wingtips and pink legs, though the goslings of both are very similar.

Snow goose (adult, blue phase)
                (immature)
                (adult, white phase)

DUCKS

Oldsquaw   *Clangula hyemalis*   A'hauanerk (L.44.5 to 59.7 cm.)
Harlequin duck   *Histrionicus histrionicus*   (L.38.1 to 44.5 cm.)

Next to the eider, the *oldsquaw* is the most likely duck to be seen. The male duck with its long needle-pointed tail (male only), dark front, white underparts and cheeks and all-dark wings, is very vocal and its sound is echoed in the Eskimo name. It breeds all over the arctic, though it rarely nests in the park area. Six to eight olive to buffy-yellow eggs are laid on the ground, often under bushes or tufts of grass.

The little *harlequin duck* may be seen in Cumberland Gulf since it certainly breeds on the southern shore. The male, a dark blue-grey duck with rufous sides and white markings on the head, neck and wings, is quite easily recognized. It often swims with its long tail cocked, bobbing its head slightly with each stroke.

EIDER DUCKS

Common eider   *Somateria mollissima*   Miterk   (L.50.8 to 66 cm.)
King eider   *Somateria spectabilis*   Kingalik (L.57.7 to 61 cm.)

Visitors to the park are sure to see great flocks, numbering in the hundreds, of these large sea-ducks flying in long low lines over the water, often alternately flapping and sailing. Migrations through Pangnirtung and Kingnait Passes are frequent and large numbers of these birds may head across Baffin Island to Greenland in late summer.

All ducks use some of their fine breast-down for nest linings, but eider down is the finest and warmest of all. Some attempts have

Red-breasted merganser (male)
Oldsquaw (male)
Harlequin duck (male)

been made on southern Baffin to create an eider-down industry—so far unsuccessfully.

The *common eiders* breed colonially, usually near the coasts and particularly west of the park. The males usually leave the flock after the eggs (olive-buff and up to six in number) are laid. The nest, on the ground and entirely lined with down, is generally near salt water, sheltered by rock piles or depressions in the low vegetation. The male is easily distinguished as it is the only duck with a *black belly* and *white back*. It has a white breast and forepart of the wing, white head with a black crown, and a long sloping frontal shield. The female is dark brown with heavily black-barred breast, and is very similar to the female king eider. Only the bill, which in the common extends twice as far up the head above the nostril as does that of the female king, is a distinguishing feature at close quarters.

The *king eider* male is the only duck with a *black back* and belly and *white foreparts*. Its large white wing-patches and heavy orange shielded bill make easy field marks. The king eider is not colonial and prefers freshwater areas for nesting, sometimes on flat tundra far from the water. The nest is lined with down, much darker than that of the common, and the four to seven eggs, similar in colour, are slightly smaller.

MERGANSERS

Red-breasted merganser   *Mergus serrator*   Paik (L.50.8 to 63.5 cm.)

The red-breasted merganser is quite rare. This fish-eating, diving duck with its long thin red bill (serrated on the sides), is distinguished by a glossy green-black head with its pronounced shaggy crest, black back, rusty chest-patch separated from the head by a

Common eider (female)
Common eider (male)
King eider (male)

large white collar, and light underparts. The female is grey, with crested rufous head.

All ducks, and their eggs, have been used as an important source of summer food by the Inuit. (See illustration p. 149.)

FALCONS

Gyrfalcon   *Falco rusticolus*   Kingavik (L.53.3 to 57.2 cm.;
  female 55.9 to 62.2 cm.)
Peregrine falcon   *Falco peregrinus*   Kingaviarsuk (L.38.1 to 45.7
  cm.; female 45.7 to 54.4 cm.)

Almost exterminated in more accessible regions by poisonous insecticides, these falcons have found a sanctuary in our arctic region. Thus it is vital to protect them here. Their only enemy is criminal man. Fines seem quite useless in preventing hunters from capturing them.

The *gyrfalcon* is large with a deceptively slow wingbeat but nonetheless a fast flight. The colour of the plumage is variable, ranging from a uniform white phase in the eastern high arctic and Greenland to a black phase in Ungava and western Canada. It is easily distinguished in its pale phase from the snowy owl by its smaller head, narrower pointed wings, and more rapid wingbeat. The facial markings are pale and the stout legs are feathered in front more than halfway to the toes.

Smaller than the gyrfalcon, the *peregrine falcon* occurs in greater numbers in the park. A crow-sized falcon, it is the most streamlined of our hawks, with long pointed wings and narrow barred tail tipped with white. When perched, the blackish cap and conspicuous facial "sideburns", dark slate-blue back and barred underparts are diagnostic. With its powerful, rapid wingstrokes, it is extremely fast in flight, and when diving for prey has been clocked at speeds of up to 180 miles per hour.

Both falcons nest on usually inaccessible cliffs inland or by the

Peregrine falco

sea, laying three to five eggs, creamy in colour with markings of rufous brown. Their nest sites can be spotted by the guano and rich nitrophilous vegetation below, and by remains of their prey: arctic hare, ptarmigan, lemmings and ducks. They are early nesters (May), the young hatching around mid-June and remaining up to seven weeks in the eyrie.

Gyrfalcon

GROUSE

Rock ptarmigan   *Lagopus mutus*   Agiki (L.32.4 to 39.4 cm.)

Who added a "P" to the good Gaelic word, *tarmachan*? This small arctic representative of the grouse family is the same species that inhabits the high Scottish hills. Its relative, the willow ptarmigan, only penetrates to Baffin's west coast.

The low rattling croak of these birds can be heard high up in the mountains, even up to 1,000 metres, but on the whole they nest on lower ground, in a depression lined with vegetation and feathers, usually sheltered by low vegetation or rocky hummocks. Their eggs, a creamy buff heavily splotched with dark brown, number usually from six to nine. In winter ptarmigan are pure white with black tails, and the males have a black bar extending from the bill through the eye—often the only detectable field mark against the snow. In summer, plumage is a light mottled brown with white wings. The males stay pure white until June, but the hen soon sports a wonderfully camouflaged plumage early in spring, and as she sits tight on her nest, it is extremely difficult to spot her before the chicks hatch. The chicks scatter as soon as they are out of the eggs, at which time the parents will perform distractive broken-wing acts to lead interlopers away from their area.

Ptarmigan eat berries and leaves, particularly of the crowberry and bilberry—and taste fine themselves!

Rock ptarmigan (male, winter)
(male, summer)

CRANE

Sandhill crane   *Grus canadensis*   Tatigak (L.86.4 to 121.9 cm.,
    wingspan 203.2 cm.)

The sandhill crane is a very large, long-legged wading bird of uniform colouration. Adults are grey, with a bare red cap and long
back-feathers which curl down over the wings and tail. Immatures
are brown. In flight, the fully extended neck, long trailing legs, and
wing motion (alternately flapping and gliding with a rapid up-
stroke) are diagnostic. The voice is a deep loud rolling rattle repeated several times.

   Although it nests to the north (Pond Inlet, Bylot Island area) the
sandhill crane might be seen in the park area, but it must be regard-
ed as a very rare visitor.

Sandhill crane

PLOVERS

Ringed plover   *Charadrius hiaticula*   Kudlikaliak (L.19.1 cm.)
Semi-palmated plover   *Charadrius semipalmatus*   Kudlikaliak
   (L.16.5 to 19.6 cm.)
Ruddy turnstone   *Arenaria interpres*   Tillivak (L.20.3 to 25.1
   cm.)

The *ringed* and the *semi-palmated plovers,* resembling smaller editions of the killdeer (but with one instead of the killdeer's two black collars), may be seen on beaches and gravelly flats. The two species are indistinguishable except in the hand. Both have brown backs, white underparts and dark yellow legs. The semi-palmated has *two* partial webs between its three toes, the ringed plover *one* small web only. The nest is a mere depression on a gravelly area, usually with four buffy spotted eggs.

The *ruddy turnstone* is rarer, but a possible visitor to the park. Its name derives from its habit of turning over beach material in search of food. A sturdy, stocky shorebird, it has orange legs and slightly upturned dark bill, strong black-and-white facial and breast markings, and in flight a striking pattern of russet, black and white on the wings and back.

SANDPIPERS

Purple sandpiper   *Erolia maritima*   (L.20.6 to 24.1 cm.)
White-rumped sandpiper   *Erolia fuscicollis*   (L.17.3 to 20.3
   cm.)
Baird's sandpiper   *Erolia bairdii*   Twitwi (L.17.3 to 19.3 cm.)

Three species of sandpipers are possibles in the park. These small "waders" are always hard to differentiate, especially in autumn plumage. Summer plumage makes it slightly easier.

A dark chunky sandpiper with short yellow legs, the *purple sandpiper's* bill is yellow at the base and slightly longer than the head, and its breast heavily streaked in breeding plumage. It is quite tame. Its nest is a depression in the ground or moss, lined with leaves of dwarf birch. It lays four eggs (greenish or buffy, with brown spots). Voice: *wee-wit.*

Purple sandpiper
Ruddy turnstone (male)
White-rumped sandpiper
Baird's sandpiper
Semi-palmated plover (male)

The *white-rumped sandpiper* is a small, streaked "peep" with a *white rump*, especially conspicuous in flight—its best field mark. The bill is straight, about the same length as the head. Its nest is usually built on a hummock in moist tundra, a slight depression lined with grasses. Its eggs, usually four, are olivey-buff splotched with browns. Voice: a thin *jeet*.

Baird's sandpiper has buffy upper parts and breast, scaly pattern on back, blackish and rather short bill and blackish legs. Its folded wings extend well beyond the tail. This small "peep" is a common inland bird farther north on Baffin. Its Eskimo name, *twitwi*, imitates its call. Its nest is a shallow depression on the ground and it usually lays four eggs (buffy with brown spots).

PHALAROPES

Red phalarope   *Phalaropus fulicarius*   Suggak (L.19.6 to 22.9 cm.)

Northern phalarope   *Lobipes lobatus*   Suggak (L.16.5 to 20.3 cm.)

Phalaropes are small, swimming sandpiper-like shorebirds, with long necks and legs and lobed toes. They often swim in small buoyant circles, spinning like tops as they dab for food. The female is the larger, more colourful of the two, takes the courtship initiative and leaves the male to incubate the eggs and care for the young.

The *northern phalarope* female, in breeding plumage, is grey above and has white underparts, a rufous-red bib and a white throat. The black bill is needle-thin and longer than that of the red. Males are duller and browner than the females.

The *red phalarope* female in breeding plumage has a white face-patch, and entire rufous-red underparts from its blackish throat to the tip of its tail. The black-tipped bill is yellow, shorter and thicker than that of other phalaropes. It is difficult to distinguish between autumn phalaropes. The different shape of the bills is diagnostic. Either of these two phalaropes may be seen in the park, though the northern is more likely. Its nest, usually a depression in a grassy tussock near a pond or marsh, is lined with grass or leaves, and the eggs, usually four, are olive-buff splotched with brown.

Northern phalarope (male)
Northern phalarope (female)
Red phalarope (female)

JAEGERS

Pomarine jaeger   *Stercorarius pomarinus*   Ishungak (L.50.8 to 58.4 cm.)
Parasitic jaeger   *Stercorarius parasiticus*   Ishungak (L.50.8 to 58.4 cm.)
Long-tailed jaeger   *Stercorarius longicaudus*   Ishungak (L.50.8 to 58.4 cm.)

These dark, falcon-like predatory sea-birds are uncommon in our area though the three species breed and range on Baffin Island. Though confusing and difficult birds to identify, their distinctive silhouette, slender wings sharply angled at the joint, the *flash of white* at the base of the primaries created by white wing quills, the hawk-like hooked beaks, and the two projecting central tail-feathers help to distinguish jaegers from gulls and terns. Remaining mostly at sea, except to nest, these are piratical birds, relentlessly pursuing others in the air and forcing them to drop their food. They occasionally range the ground seeking and eating lemmings, young birds and eggs. They are ground nesters, usually laying two olive-brownish spotted eggs.

With considerable colour variation, the only sure means of identifying live specimens is by their tails (see illustration). The *parasitic jaeger* adult has *short, flat, pointed* central tail-feathers projecting 1.3 to 9.4 centimetres. The *pomarine jaeger* has *broad twisted*, usually *stubby* central tail-feathers, projecting about 2.5 to 10.2 centimetres. The *long-tailed jaeger* has central tail-feathers extending 12.7 to 22.9 centimetres beyond the others.

All immatures lack the long tail-feathers.

Tails of Jaegers

Pomarine jaeger

Parasitic jaeger

Long-tailed jaeger

Parasitic jaeger

GULLS

Glaucous gull   *Larus hyperboreus*   Nauyak (L.66 to 76.2 cm.)
Iceland gull   *Larus glaucoides*   Nauyak (L.58.4 to 63.5 cm.)
Herring gull   *Larus argentatus*   Nauyak (L.58 to 66 cm.)
Black-legged kittiwake   *Rissa tridactyla*   Nauyava (L.40.6 to
   45.7 cm.)
Sabine's gull   *Xema sabini*   (L.33 to 35.6 cm.)

The commonest gull in Cumberland Peninsula is the *glaucous*. One
of the largest gulls, its white wingtips distinguish it from the slightly
smaller *herring gull* and its size from the even smaller *Iceland gull*.
The latter two are rare occurrences in the park. The glaucous,
though very similar in colour to the Iceland, has a heavier and
longer bill, and at very close range a narrow *yellow* eye-ring, while
the Iceland's eye-ring is *red*. The mantles of both glaucous and Iceland adults are *very pale* grey and the primaries *always white*, compared to the darker grey mantle and black wingtips of the herring.
All of these gulls have flesh-pink legs and take several years to
attain their full adult plumage, remaining speckly brown while
juvenile. Second year glaucous are pure white throughout. The
glaucous gulls nest, often in colonies, on rocky ledges and small
islets, making a messy grass-mud affair of a nest, and laying two or
three eggs, buffy-brown to olive-brown, splotched with dark
brown. The young wander and swim long before achieving flight
capability, so the families are still around into the second half of
August. They generally feed on small fish and carrion but are far
from averse to taking other young birds and eggs.

Herring gull (immature)
Herring gull (adult)
Glaucous gull (immature)
Glaucous gull (adult)

North of the park (but not in our area) are breeding stations of the *black-legged kittiwake* and *Sabine's gull*. Both have been noted in the park but must be considered unusual. Their small size and *black* legs, as well as the kittiwake's clearly defined triangular wingtips of *solid black*, and the Sabine's' strongly forked tail and *black head* (summer plumage), distinguish these two from other northern gull species.

Sabine's gull
Fulmar
Kittiwake

AUKS (ALCIDS)

Thick-billed murre   *Uria lomvia*   Aqpa (L.43.2 to 48.3 cm.)
Dovekie   *Plautus alle*   (L.19.1 to 22.9 cm.)
Black guillemot   *Cepphus grylle*   Pitsiolak (L.30.5 to 35.6 cm.)

These black and white pelagic birds, with their short tails and short narrow wings, somewhat resemble penguins as they stand in crowded colonies on their nesting sites. When flying, they circle and veer with very rapid wing-beats. Usually remaining at sea, where they use their wings to swim underwater, they come ashore only to breed.

The *thick-billed murre* (or Brunnich's murre) is the commonest of these sea birds in this area. They establish huge breeding colonies in Reid Bay and Exeter Sound on eastern Cumberland Peninsula and thus are seen often in the park's coastal waters where they feed on small fish and crustacea. The size of a small duck, they have a pointed bill which has a white streak near the gape, black head, back and wings, and white underparts. Nesting on sea cliff ledges they lay a single egg (most often bluish-green splotched with brown) that is pear-shaped, so that (with luck!) it will not roll off the ledge. At sea their rapid wing-beat is diagnostic, and they will often dive when approached by boat. They have been used to supplement the native diet in summer; the eggs and flesh make excellent eating.

The little *dovekie* might be seen in Davis Strait waters by late season visitors. This tiny black and white alcid breeds in northwest Greenland and perhaps Ellesmere Island, travelling south only as far as it must to find open water. It is easily identified by its tiny size, its short, stubby and neckless appearance, its very small bill, and its rapidly whirring wing-beats.

The *black guillemot* is black with large *white wing-patches* (the only alcid to have them). The bill is rather long, pointed and black, and the legs are red. It is less gregarious than the other alcids and nests in rock crevices and crannies on steep coasts, laying two pointed, whitish eggs blotched with browns and greys. It is even more likely to be seen in the southern area of the park than the murre, as it sports in the fiords.

Thick-billed murre
Black guillemot
Dovekie

OWLS

Snowy owl   *Nyctea scandiaca*   Ookpik. . .juak (L.55.9 to 68.6 cm.; female larger than male)

No one should have any difficulty recognizing this large bird, the only Baffin representative of its family. Snowy owl numbers depend greatly on lemming abundance. In 1953 Watson had the good fortune to make a detailed study of these birds in Owl Valley. Eggs, up to nine, are incubated as soon as laid, hence the young are of startlingly different size, and the youngest owls are lucky if they survive. Nests are sometimes on the ground but more often on top of large boulders. Near the nest these birds are quite aggressive and an unhelmeted observor is advised to keep his distance!

LARKS

Horned lark   *Eremophila alpestris*   Tinged-luktuk (L.17.3 to 20.3 cm.)

Larks are slender-billed, brown ground-birds, larger than a sparrow, that *run* or walk energetically instead of hopping. Watch for the strong facial pattern, black "whiskers" curving from the bill back under the eyes, and the broad black bib-patch under the yellow throat. The tiny black "horns" of the male are not always visible. Females are duller, but show the horned lark pattern. Flight is rather undulating, and when seen from below the black of the tail contrasts with the white underparts. The face and breast-pattern as well as the yellow throat and black tail-feathers help distinguish the lark from the slightly smaller pipit. Horned larks nest on the ground, even up to considerable altitudes (750 metres), and the nest

Snowy owl

of grasses and leaves contains up to five greyish eggs speckled with pale brown. They often give their tinkling staccato song high overhead, as well as on the ground. They are one of the rarest of the small inland birds that breed on Baffin. (See illustration p. 177.)

CROWS

Raven   *Corvus corax*   Tulugak (L.55.9 to 67.3 cm.)

There should be no difficulty recognizing this bird which is pure black, and the only Baffin representative of its family. Ravens, which like the snowy owl can be seen at any time of year, are carrion eaters and scavengers, and are now often concentrated at village dumps. Heavier than the crow, their flight is more hawk-like as they alternately flap and soar on *horizontal* wings (crows bend wings upwards). Their ample wedge-shaped tail, heavy bill and shaggy throat-feathers are diagnostic. They are very early nesters, laying four to five eggs in April, in nests made of sticks, on usually inaccessible cliff ledges. They delight in aerobatics and their hoarse croak is often recognizable before the birds are seen. Away from villages they are uncommon, except on the Kivitoo peninsula.

Raven

THRUSHES

Wheatear   *Oenanthe oenanthe*   Erkoligak (L. 14 to 15.2 cm.)

Wheatears are rare in the park. Though they breed in the eastern
Arctic, they prefer to winter in the Old World, leaving Baffin early
to set out on their long autumn journey. Small, restless ground
birds, seldom still, they hop along on the ground, constantly bobbing, spreading and pumping their tails. Adult males are grey
above, buffy-white below, and the wings are black. Watch for the
distinctive white of the *rump-patch* and *base of tail*, terminating in
a broad black inverted "T". The adult male has a black patch across
the face, beneath the eye, and a white stripe above it. The female
lacks the face-patch and is generally more cinnamon-brownish in
colour. Locating its nest will be a real triumph, as it tends to hide it
under rocks, in crevices, or in holes in the ground. The nest itself is
rather flimsy, usually made of grass or moss, lined with feathers,
hair, plant wool, and such materials, in which it lays five to seven
pale blue eggs. Voice: a strong *chack-chack*, and a song that is a
rather melodious warble.

PIPITS

Water pipit   *Anthus spinoletta*   Siusiuk (L.15.2 to 17.8 cm.)

The pipit is a small, sparrow-sized bird with a slender bill, light
eye-stripe, brownish back, buffy underparts darkly streaked on the
breast, blackish legs, and white outer tail-feathers. It *walks* rather
than hops, and *wags its tail* constantly. For nesting, it prefers dry
slopes (such as in Owl Valley) rather than flatlands, and lays four
to six eggs (greyish or buffy-white thickly spotted with browns) in a
grass-lined nest. The young are fed until early August. Voice: in
flight, a sharp *tsip-tsip* or *tsip-it* (hence "pipit"). Near the nesting
site it gives a tinkling flight song. It is perhaps the third commonest bird of the interior (the other two being the snow bunting and
the Lapland longspur).

Horned lark (male)
Wheatear (male)
Water pipit

FINCHES AND SPARROWS

Hoary redpoll   *Acanthis hornemanni*   Sakoariak (L.11.4 to 15.2 cm.)
Common redpoll   *Acanthis flammea*   Sakoariak (L.11.4 to 15.2 cm.)

The two species of redpoll are found in the same habitat, often on old lateral moraines. The common, as its name implies, is in the majority. Both species nest in low, shrubby ground-cover or birch if available, laying up to six pale blue, reddish-spotted eggs. The nest may be used more than one year and is made of grasses and weed-stems, and is warmly lined with mountain avens seed-wool, cottony plant down, feathers, fur and hair.

The *common redpoll* is a small, streaky, grey-brown finch with a jaunty ruby-red cap perched over its eyes, and a tiny square black bib under its stubby finch-bill (it is a seed-eater). It has two narrow white wing-bars and a deeply notched tail. The back is dusky grey, overlaid with indistinct frosty grey-white and darker grey streaks. The rump is greyish-white, heavily streaked with dark. The *males* are red or pink-breasted, and also often have a pinkish tinge on cheeks, sides and rump. *Females* are similar to males but lack the pink suffusion.

The *hoary redpoll* is very similar to the common. The only reliable field mark is the *white, unstreaked* rump and its generally paler, frostier look. Voice: flight call is a double-noted *chit-chit*, song, a trill and a twitter. Flocks keep up a constant twittering in flight.

Lapland longspur   *Calcarius lapponicus*   Kowlegak (L. 15.2 to 17.8 cm.)
Snow bunting   *Plectrophenax nivalis*   Kopanoark (L.15.2 to 18.8 cm.)

Finally, we come to our two commonest small bird species, the

Lapland longspur (female)
Lapland longspur (male)
Hoary redpoll (male)
Common redpoll (male)

Lapland longspur and the snow bunting. In breeding plumage the males of the two species are easily distinguished, especially as their nesting habitats are quite different. The longspurs choose low, wet, hummocky areas with sedgy tundra cover, while the buntings prefer to nest in bouldery terrain, even high up in the mountains.

The *longspur* males in breeding plumage are easily identified by the *black crown, face* and *breast*, a broad buff stripe behind the eye, and a *chestnut* patch on the nape of the neck. The tail is blackish with mostly *white* outer tail-feathers. The hind toenail is as long, or longer, than the hind toe (hence "longspur"). The yellow bill is short and stubby like a sparrow's. The back is buffy, heavily striped with black, and the underparts are white streaked with black on the flanks. Females are more nondescript. You will see quantities of these little sparrow-like ground birds in July and early August, running and occasionally hopping along the ground, and at that time the females and young are more difficult to distinguish. Their nest is of grasses lined with willow cotton, feathers and fine grasses, and placed in or under a tussock of grass or low shrubs. It contains four to six greenish-grey to olive-brown eggs, splotched with browns and black. Flight-call: a two- or three-syllable dry rattle, but over the breeding ground the male sings a cheerful short warbling song as he drifts down to the ground on set wings.

The *snow bunting* is a sturdy ground finch. In breeding plumage (so very different from the "down south" buntings we know), the cock bunting is a handsome *pure white* with a smartly contrasting-*black back, bill* and *legs*. Inner tail-feathers are also black, the rest white. Wings appear mostly white with black tips. In its undulating flight, watch for this flashing white wing-patch, and the overall black-and-white pattern. Overhead they look almost entirely white, like a flock of snowflakes. The female is similar to the male but has a less definite black-and-white pattern, and a distinct rusty tinge, especially on top of her head. For nesting sites the buntings choose crevices and crannies in rocks, cliff faces, or under stone piles. The nest is made of grasses and mosses and lined with grasses, hair, feathers, and so on. In it they lay four to seven eggs (greyish- or bluish-white splotched with lavender and browns). In flight the voice is a short musical twitter, which often ends in an abrupt

Snow bunting (male)
(female)

chert. Over or on the breeding grounds it sings a loud pleasant warble.

The arrival and song of the snow buntings heralds the onslaught of the arctic summer. When they depart, the last migrants to leave, the short, hectic season is definitely over.

References

Godfrey, W.E. *Birds of Canada*. Ottawa: Queen's Printer, 1966.
Peterson, R.T. *A Field Guide to the Birds*. Markham, Ont.: Houghton Mifflin of Canada, 1947.
Watson, A. "Birds in Cumberland Peninsula" in *Canadian Field Naturalist* 71 (1957): 87-109.

The Mammals

In the park area and its neighbouring seas there can be found only nine land mammal and perhaps only eight sea mammal species. These are as follows in approximate order of likely occurrence:

On Land

Brown lemming	*Lemmus sibiricus*	Avingaq
Collared lemming	*Dicrostonyx torquatus*	Avingaq
Ermine	*Mustela erminea*	Tiriak
Arctic hare	*Lepus arcticus*	Ukalik
Arctic fox	*Alopex lagopus*	Tiriganiak
Caribou	*Rangifer tarandus*	Tuktu
Polar bear	*Ursus maritimus*	Nanuk
Wolf	*Canis lupus*	Amaruk
Wolverine	*Gulo gulo*	Kapvik

At Sea

Ringed seal	*Phoca hispida*	Natsia
Bearded seal	*Erignathus barbatus*	Ujjuk
White whale	*Delphinapterus leucas*	Qilalu
Walrus	*Odobenus rosmarus*	Aivik
Narwhal	*Monodon monoceros*	Qilaluga
Killer whale	*Orcinus orca*	Arluk
Bowhead whale	*Balaena mysticetus*	Arvik
Humpbacked whale	*Megaptera novaeangliae*	Arvik

Land Mammals

Lemmings *may* be the animal most often seen in the park but their numbers vary tremendously from year to year. In 1953, Pangnirtung Pass was crawling with them—in other years there have been very few.

There are two species here: the brown lemming and the collared lemming. The latter has a dark stripe down the back and turns white in winter. It seems to prefer drier heath slopes. Lemmings are usually shy and vanish rapidly down their shallow burrows when disturbed. Small wonder! They are preyed on by ermine, foxes, owls and other predatory birds, and hence are the unhappy link in the food chain. When their numbers are great they can cause serious damage to vegetation, unless there is at the same time an exceptional influx of predators.

The ermine is the only weasel in our area. In summer it has a brown back and white belly and is pure white only in winter—even then it has a black-tipped tail. It is an inquisitive fellow, and by sitting still one can often tempt it to approach within very close range. The southern part of Pangnirtung Pass was named Weasel Valley because of the ermine's disturbing habit of running over tent-roofs.

The arctic hare and arctic fox can be seen throughout the park, often in quite high and apparently barren locations. Surprising to southern visitors is their relative size: the hare (which weighs up to five kilograms) is usually heavier than the fox, smallest of his breed. Both are pure white in winter, but are patchy grey-brown on the back in summer. The hare is, of course, a herbivore; the fox eats anything from lemmings to small birds and their eggs. In winter he is often a scavenging follower of the polar bear.

The largest and only potentially dangerous animal, the polar bear is a rarity in the park. Essentially seal hunters, bears tend to wander inland only in the fall when tempted by berries. Traces have been seen high (1,200 metres) on glaciers within the park, but they are most likely to be seen on the northern coasts, in the Kivitoo region for example. It is wise to give polar bears a wide berth, especially females with cubs, but as with most bears, loud noises are usually sufficient to discourage them.

Caribou are rare within the park boundaries though antlers found in Pangnirtung Pass bear witness to the former presence. Today they will be found only in the northwest corner of the park and outside its boundary to the southwest, stragglers from the Baffin Island herd which occupies the lower ground in the central and western parts of the island. The wolf is a follower of the caribou herd, though like most predators it will often feed on lemmings, especially when they are abundant.

Few park visitors will see a wolverine, though this largest of the weasel family may be present. It, too, is an inhabitant of the western parts of the island. A notorious raider of food caches, it is most unpopular. The wolverine fur has a quality which makes it the finest trimming for parka hoods, as frost and ice from the moist breath of the wearer will not accumulate on it.

Sea Mammals

Most park visitors will have made at least a short sea journey to reach it, and thus have had the opportunity to observe some of the life of the water, always more important to the original inhabitants than the life on land. The two seals most likely to be seen differ greatly in size: the rarer bearded seal weighs up to 250 kilograms; besides its bulk, its bristly mustaches may help to differentiate it from the ringed seal.

White whales are quite common in Cumberland Gulf, particularly toward Clearwater Fiord. In former days, a considerable trade in white whale hide was carried out at Pangnirtung; these skins were shipped to England to be made into the highest quality bootlaces.

Narwhal and walrus are rarer and are most likely to be seen on the northern coasts of Cumberland Peninsula, as is the killer whale. Now comparatively familiar to people since its introduction into "marinelands", this whale's high dorsal fin and black-and-white marking distinguish it from the baleen whale. These latter appear to be making a slow comeback in numbers in arctic waters and sightings are on the increase.

The bowhead whale has *no* dorsal fin, the humpback a small one well back on the body as well as long knobby pectoral fins which are often exposed when this playful monster surfaces.

References

This description of the mammals of Auyuittuq has been necessarily brief. The following references will be of help to those who wish more information:

Banfield, A.W.F., *The Mammals of Canada*. National Museum of Natural Sciences. Toronto: University of Toronto Press, 1974. 405 pp., illus.

Kelsall, J.P. *The Caribou*. Canadian Wildlife Service. Ottawa: The Queen's Printer, 1968. Cat. no. R 65-7/3. 340 pp., maps, illus.

Peterson, Randolph L. *The Mammals of Eastern Canada*. Royal Ontario Museum, Toronto: Oxford University Press, 1966. 465 pp., illus.

4. Aids to the Park Visitor

Patrick Baird

Access

Travel to this arctic mountain park is not easy: it can't be reached by automobile or camper, and visitors are advised to plan in advance.

The latest information on park regulations and local travel facilities can be obtained only from the park's superintendent at Pangnirtung. Generally speaking however:

1. There is regular commercial air transport several times a week to Pangnirtung and less frequently to Broughton Island, both of which have airfields capable of handling planes up to the size of the DC-3.

2. At both settlements there is limited commercial accommodation, and campgrounds have been provided for which a small fee is payable to the local councils.

3. Further travel by air, boat or freighter canoe is dependent on ice conditions. Ice usually prevents ship arrivals in the region until at least mid-July, and boating operations are uncertain at Pangnirtung until then and later on the northern coast. Pangnirtung Pass (altitude 390 metres) usually becomes ice-free during the last days of July, but ice *has* persisted there through August. Water transport from Pangnirtung can be arranged by freighter canoe or motorboat, and from Broughton Island similar charters can take the visitor to the northern fiords when ice conditions permit.

4. Until late June the frozen surfaces of fiords and lakes allow transport by motorized sled, and depots of provisions can be arranged by this means. Loaded sleds, however, are seldom able to negotiate Weasel Valley, and access to Summit Lake by sled has to be by the much longer route from the north.

5. Helicopter or light aircraft charter may be available, but enquiries regarding such services should be made well in advance.

6. Food and fuel (white gas and kerosene), including freeze-dried products, *should* be available at Hudson's Bay Company stores at Pangnirtung or Broughton. But because the beginning of the hiking-climbing season comes before the annual sea-lift, it is wise to check on supplies and order them beforehand.

Hiking and Mountaineering in the Park

To appreciate the attractions of Auyuittuq National Park one might take a two-hour flight over and around it. But the only way to make real contact with its beauty is to tread the surface, sleep on it, see it from close up, and best of all, to climb some of the heights, whereby the intimate touch and the distant view are combined.

Arctic hiking is quite a bit different and more difficult than walking through other areas of the Canadian wilderness. First, there are none of the trees which further south provide shelter, fuel, and materials for bridge building. Here there are only large overhanging boulders—fortunately in plentiful supply—to give shelter from the wind and wet. Strong wind combined with rain or wet snow at near the freezing point—conditions which can occur in every month of the year—has caused more exposure casualties than full winter cold. To keep dry is to keep warm—sometimes even to survive. One favorable arctic phenomenon, however, is the long summer day, twenty-four-hour daylight from early May until well into August.

But until he has adjusted to the scale of things, the traveller can be misled by clear air on fine days into underestimating distances and heights, and hence travel time.

The hiker, and even more so the mountaineer, intending a stay in the field for some length of time, will be encumbered to varying degrees. Even with a light load, a fit walker will have difficulty averaging more than three kilometres per hour on a full day's march. There will be many different types of ground to traverse (and water and maybe snow). Extensive gravelly flats provide the best going,

Fig. 60. Aerial view of Auyuittuq peaks.

but beware of following them too far towards a river bar as they may deteriorate into wetter and deeper sand. Dry tundra ridges may be bouldery but provide fair going, but if possible, avoid the yellow tint of deep mossy tundra into which a laden person's steps will sink as into foot-deep snow. You will never entirely be able to avoid Baffin's glacial moraines, where side glaciers have thrust down into the main valleys. These obstacles may be scores of metres high, made up of rough, angular boulders, and the walker must balance carefully to avoid ankle-wrenching or skin-breaking falls.

River Crossings

There will always be rivers to cross and no material available to bridge them, unless in the spring and early summer the bridging has been accomplished by snow and/or ice. During the glacier melt season, which is strongest in July, streams originating from the glaciers can be large, cold, and turbulent and pose crossing problems. Keep your footwear dry, and avoid injury. Do not succumb to the temptation to head uphill where you think you can leap from bank to boulder to bank, a manoeuvre which might result in a ducking or an injured leg. Aim for the widest, shallowest spots, or for places where the river divides into several streams. Remove boots, socks and maybe trousers and wade barefoot, or better still put on running shoes, for your feet can lose feeling quickly in the near-freezing water and cause a stumble.

A quick knee- or even thigh-deep wade, aided preferably by an ice axe or ski pole as a balancer, and you will be drying cool feet and putting on warm socks and boots. On occasion no detour of a reasonable length will reveal a non-turbulent reach of the stream. In this case, link arms or hold ski poles or axes horizontally together and wade abreast with the strongest member of the party upstream.

Snow and Ice

A feature of glacial Baffin Island is *aufeis*—large flat areas of layered ice up to several metres thick caused by water continuing to flow and flood when severely cold conditions prevail. Quite often these ice-covered areas may last throughout the summer in wide valley reaches. They provide excellent walking, but care must be taken that sub-ice streams have not weakened what seems to be a firm surface. They may provide bridges over large rivers in the early summer, as will winter-drifted snow, but these should be treated with care and a rope used as a safeguard for at least the first person across.

The glaciers themselves, of course, provide good walking surfaces. Where the ice is bare of snow any crevasse is visible, but on higher reaches of the glaciers, where winter snow has lingered, the usual mountaineering precautions should be taken. Baffin crevasses do, however, tend to be fewer and narrower than those on temperate region glaciers.

Clothing and Shelter

A few hints will suffice to make life easier for the Baffin walker. Surely it can be assumed that those who embark on an arctic hike are already familiar with lightweight gear, backpacking technique, and the care of feet. Windproof clothing is essential. Winds in Pangnirtung Pass can reach gale force at any time of year. Take a down jacket for camp and a gale-proof tent, and remember that at

Fig. 61. Park wardens in Pangnirtung Pass during a training course in lifesaving techniques.

all times open boat or canoe travel is extremely cold and you need all your clothing *and* a spray-proof outer cover. A light, hooded jacket is also convenient for protection against the attacks of mosquitoes. These are the only biting insects likely to be encountered within this area of Baffin and are moderately troublesome on calm, warm days; but the arctic mosquito is large and slow-moving—one can take satisfying reprisals against it. As mentioned above, running shoes for wading and a ski pole or axe are helpful. You may have to traverse long stretches of snow or ice even in midsummer, so dark glasses should be carried, as well as some kind of waterproof cagoule and a waterproof cover for that treasured sleeping bag, and for your matches.

Unless you are headed for the Penny Ice Cap, a compass is not of much value since mountain walls define your movements fairly rigorously. But do use a map. Descending the wrong glacier can lead to many extra miles of walking.

The selection of camp sites poses certain problems. The fragility of local vegetation means that traffic on and around a camp occupied for a long period or by a large number can be destructive. On the other hand, camping on a sand plain can be miserable: when the wind blows everything, including dinner, may be sand-blasted. Try to pick a *small* sand or gravel area or a dry, well-grassed site near a freshwater stream. You *can* drink the heavily silted glacial outflows but lengthy use of this water can cause digestive upset.

Make a stone-walled cooking shelter and be sure that fire cannot get into an extensive area of arctic heather. The disposal of wastes in this arctic park must be carefully planned. Latrine pits can be dug in sand but not very deeply as the permanently frozen ground is often quite close to the surface. In order to preserve the cleanliness of the park for future visitors, all garbage that cannot be burned should be carried out.

Pangnirtung Pass is probably the route that will be used most by hikers as well as by mountaineers heading for a climbing base. In order to preserve the park's wilderness, authorities plan to erect only those facilities necessary for safety. Nevertheless, a description of the easiest ways to negotiate this finest of Canadian arctic passes may be helpful. Nowhere in the world can one find a more spectacular entry into the Arctic Circle (Lat. 66° 33' N.), Mount Odin on the west and Mount Thor on the east serving as fantastically beautiful gateposts.

Fig. 62. Typical glacier stream in Pangnirtung Pass.

Pangnirtung Pass

At the head of South Pangnirtung Fiord, where the tidal range is considerable, there is a typical braided glacier stream outflow. This results in diffuse channels and sandbars alternately exposed and covered as the tide ebbs and flows. The east (left) bank provides the best take-off for walking up-pass and here below Overlord Peak is the park warden's hut and a campground. The glacial tributary streams on this side are not too difficult to ford, whereas on the west (right) bank Crater Lake's outflow can be troublesome and a large river descends from the spectacular Schwartzenbach Falls two-and-one-half kilometres above Crater Lake.

Walk up the east bank of Weasel River, first over ten kilometres of gravel flats and then over the sand dunes and green, grassy slopes below Tirokwa (Corner) Peak. This is a pleasant hike, unless you are too heavily laden, until you reach the moraine of Forkbeard Glacier with its two large streams. The main Weasel River can be crossed below this between Mount Sif and Mount Odin, where it is much divided into braids. But this is a cold and thigh-deep business in the summer melt season, and a few miles further upstream a large and difficult river comes in from the west from the glacier south of Mount Tyr. The aufeis-covered flats below the outlet of Summit Lake are often snow-bridged well into July, but a better crossing place of the main river is right at the outlet rapids of the lake, and a permanent wire-rope bridge has been set up there. This is about thirty-six kilometres from tidewater or twelve hours' march. One kilometre north of the lake outlet on the west shore is a shelter built in 1973 by the park authority where emergency equipment and a two-way radio are installed.

The west side of Summit Lake is an easy walk, whereas the east side is encumbered with several large moraines and giant boulder stretches. Traversing the toe of Turner Glacier brings one to Glacier Lake, which now flows into Summit Lake through a channel about twenty metres wide between sandbars. Glacier Lake's former overflow channel into Owl River dried up some time between 1953 and 1961 and the slopes of Mount Battle can be reached by walking over the moraine of Highway Glacier.

Owl Valley is wider, better vegetated, and has a gentler descent than Weasel Valley, and although once again several large tributaries enter it, especially that from Rundle Glacier, either bank makes for reasonable hiking. The use of the word "hiking" does not mean that Pangnirtung Pass should be attempted by anyone who is inex-

Fig. 63. Emergency shelter at the head of south Pangnirtung Fiord.

perienced in traversing rough mountain country. The crossing of its glacial streams requires considerable care.

Other potential hiking routes which keep to comparatively low ground are mainly outside the present park boundaries. These include the Kingnait Pass route from Kingnait Fiord to Padle Fiord where the western tributaries of both Naksakjua and June Rivers provide easy passes over to Owl River, and the region to the southwest of the park east of Shark Fiord.

In the north, within the boundaries, a good pass exists between Maktak Fiord and Narpaing or Quajon Fiords, some forty kilometres in extent.

All these latter areas house a richer tundra vegetation than Pangnirtung Pass, and the sea travel involved in reaching them gives the visitor an opportunity to observe a greater number of sea birds and mammals.

Mountaineering

The potential for mountaineering on Cumberland Peninsula was discovered in 1953, when the Arctic Institute of North America undertook a major scientific expedition to the region. This party included several experienced climbers and witnessed the first ascents of Mounts Battle, Asgard (north peak), Odin—the highest summit, and Tête Blanche.

In 1961, six mountaineers from Cambridge, England traversed the pass from north to south scaling for the first time Mounts Fleming, Freya and Friga (south summit), now renamed Iviangernat.

In 1963 and 1965, two expeditions of the Alpine Club of Canada were encamped, the first at the head of Pangnirtung Fiord and the second at Glacier Lake. On the former occasion the local minister at Pangnirtung, Reverend Sydney Wilkinson, who had performed some notable solo ascents, joined the group and ascents were made of Tirokwa, Mount Turnweather and Tête des Cirques. In 1965, Mounts Loki and Thor were among the major new climbs. In 1970, a mixed-national group from Queen's University added Mount Sif and Mount Baldur to the growing list of first ascents in the pass. Since 1970, each year has seen an increasing number of climbing expeditions operating either within the park boundaries or in neighbouring areas.

The special charm of climbing on Baffin Island has been its remoteness and solitude compared with the mountains of Europe and even the Rockies, now increasingly overcrowded and littered with trash. There is also tremendous appeal in treading a summit for the first time or tackling a huge, unmarked rock wall. Baffin abounds in both of these, though in the immediate vicinity of Pangnirtung Pass the majority of the peaks have been ascended at least once.

The rock in the park is clean granite and gneiss with only occasional locations of friable iron-rich haematite rock. The peaks rise 1,500 to 2,000 metres from the valley floors, the only 2,000-metre peaks between Ellesmere Island and North Carolina. Glaciers descend to a few hundred metres above sea level or, as in Coronation Fiord and Okoa Bay, reach the sea itself in cliff fronts.

How does climbing in this region differ from mountaineering technique in better-known ranges? First, in the summer months until mid-August there is no movement-impeding darkness. The length of an excursion is controlled, therefore, not by daylight but by the power of one's legs and adequacy of food.

"Night", however, does tend to affect snow surfaces, and in clear weather one can often tread easily between 10:00 P.M. and 10:00 A.M. on snow that would provide heavy going during the other twelve hours. Snow conditions do in fact vary enormously from year to year. In 1972, for instance, a cool summer left snow at mod-

Fig. 64. River crossing by wire-rope bridge.

erate altitudes throughout the season, whereas by early July 1974, after a remarkably snowless winter, there was scarcely any snow left below 1,200 metres, and glacier melt was very powerful. Normally these glacier-fed streams are highest at the end of July; in August there is a diminution, but the snowline can descend again during the latter half of the month and verglas on the rocks can add to climbing difficulties. In 1953, however, fine, full summer conditions still prevailed at the end of August.

The course of snow melt on the glaciers can result in large slush pools developing in the hollows on flat upper reaches. Snowshoes or light skis can be a boon, though their inclusion in your equipment must be weighed against the additional weight and awkwardness in carrying. Few parties have yet sampled the possibility of ski-mountaineering in May and June, but there are areas on and around the Penny Ice Cap and to the east of the lower Owl Valley where this sport could be indulged. The author enjoyed a splendid 1,000-metre run down from the ice cap as late as July 12. In late April 1966, Hans Weber, on his way to research on the Penny Ice Cap, enjoyed fine climbing weather to the south of the ice cap, but normally it would still be rather cold for ski activities at that date.

By 1973, nearly all the peaks close to Pangnirtung Pass had been ascended at least once, and also several in the area north of the Penny Ice Cap. Mountaineering groups have recently been very active in the region between Pangnirtung Pass and Kingnait Fiord, and also east of the latter—outside of the originally declared park boundaries.

World-wide interest has been aroused in the charms of virgin peaks and unscaled walls of over 1,000 metres in vertical height. Mountaineers from Britain, Switzerland, Italy, France and Japan have been as well represented as North Americans.

A list of ascents would be too long and ephemeral to include in this handbook, but a permanent record is kept up-to-date at the park headquarters at Pangnirtung. The references in climbing literature cited below will give an indication of what has been accomplished to date, as well as some of the peculiar problems to be faced.

References

Alpine Journal 67 (1963): 97-110.
Arctic 6 (1953): 227-251.
Canadian Alpine Journal 37 (1954): 31-33; 47 (1964): 1-15; 49 (1966): 28-42; 55 (1972): 49, 52-54; 56 (1973): 93-93; 57 (1974): 95-98.
Mountain 22: 20-25; 26: 33-35
Mountain World (1954) 147-168; (1964-5) 150-158.

Biographies

In 1934, while still a student, PATRICK BAIRD first set foot on Canadian soil, fittingly enough on Baffin Island during the first of his many trips to this area. He received his M.A. in Geology from Cambridge University in 1938 and served with the Royal Canadian Artillery and the Department of National Defense from 1939 to 1947.

In 1946 he commanded "Exercise Musk-ox", a vehicle trek which made a half circle from Churchill Manitoba, along the arctic coast, and finishing in Edmonton.

In 1953 he led the first Arctic Institute expedition to Pangnirtung Pass. As a result of this expedition, plus the eleven others he has made to Baffin Island since 1934, very few people, if any, know the Cumberland Peninsula as well as he does.

Mr. Baird is now retired but is still very active. He will be heading for Ellesmere Island in August 1976 and hopes to return to Baffin in 1977.

Born in Cheshire, England, RAYMOND S. BRADLEY received a B.Sc. at the University of Southampton, England, and an M.A. and Ph.D. at the University of Colorado, Institute of Arctic and Alpine Research. He has researched different aspects of the climate of Baffin Island, the climatic history of the western United States, recent changes in the climate of the Canadian Arctic and glacier-climate relationships, and has done several years of field work on Baffin and Ellesmere Islands. "Blue eyes, handsome, debonair, 'not just a colleague—a friend'; fond of tropical fish, ballroom dancing; has stern eyes and masculine chin; hates writing biographical notes."

Editor's note: Dr. Bradley also has a sense of humour and enjoys his work thoroughly.

Originally from Beauce County in Quebec, JEAN-LUC GRONDIN studied sculpture at the Quebec School of Fine Arts. For ten years he worked as an artist at the Quebec Zoological Gardens and contributed to a series of publications called "Les Carnets Zoologiques". A director of the Quebec Zoological Society, he has been actively engaged over a number of years as secretary of the Quebec

Ornithologists Club. He prepared the illustrations for *Les Oiseaux du Quebec* (Cayouette and Grondin, 1972). His illustrations for this book represent his first major venture into colour paintings of birds.

GIFFORD H. MILLER had his first contact with the northern lands while serving one and a half years as an anti-poverty volunteer in a small village in western Alaska. Shortly thereafter, affiliated with the University of Colorado, he began field studies on the glacial history of Cumberland Peninsula, and has spent the last six summers investigating the glacial and climatic history along eastern Baffin Island. He obtained his B.A. and Ph.D. in Geological Sciences from the University of Colorado, and is presently associated with the Geophysical Laboratory of The Carnegie Institution of Washington and the Institute of Arctic and Alpine Research at the University of Colorado.

After arriving in North America from his native Denmark, PETER SCHLEDERMANN worked in New York and later spent three years homesteading in Alaska. He then attended the University of Alaska, earning his B.A. in Anthropology and Geography in 1969. He obtained his M.A. in Anthropology from Memorial University of Newfoundland in 1971 and his Ph.D. in Archaeology from the University of Calgary in 1975.

Dr. Schledermann has worked in all areas of the Arctic including Alaska, Labrador, Baffin, Ellesmere and Banks Islands. He is currently working with the Danish National Museum on a joint project in Greenland. Dr. Schledermann is an assistant professor with the Department of Archaeology at the University of Calgary.

ROGER WILSON was born in Noranda, Quebec. He attended Queen's University and later Memorial University of Newfoundland where he received a B.Sc. (hon.) in Biology in 1968. The same year he joined Parks Canada where he worked as a seasonal naturalist at Cape Breton Highlands National Park, and then as Chief Park Naturalist at Terra Nova National Park. In 1971 he became Interpretation Specialist at the Atlantic Regional Office and in 1973 was transferred to Quebec where he assumed his present position as Assistant Chief, Interpretation, Quebec Region.

Picture Credits

Where more than one picture occurs on a page, the order of credits is left to right, top to bottom.

Cover photo   R. Vroom

Chapter 1
  Frontispiece   G.H. Miller
  Fig. 1, 2   G.H. Miller
        4   D. Le Sauteur
        5, 6, 12   M. Darry
        7   Government of Canada
        8, 9-11, 13
        15, 16, 18-20   G.H. Miller
        21   M.G. Miller
        22-24, 26   G.H. Miller

Chapter 2
  Fig. 40   Parcs Canada Québec
  All other photos   P. Schledermann

Chapter 3
  Fig. 52   D. Le Sauteur
        53   J.L. Blouin
        54   R. Wilson
        55, 56   D. Le Sauteur
        57   A. Guimond
        58   R. Wilson
        59   E. Seiber
  Pages 109-113   R. Wilson
        115   D. MacAdam
        117   D. MacAdam, R. Wilson, D. MacAdam
        119   E. Seiber, D. MacAdam
        121   D. MacAdam
        123   D. MacAdam, G. Jackson
        125   D. MacAdam, R. Wilson
        127   R. Wilson, D. MacAdam
        129   R. Wilson, E. Seiber
        131   D. MacAdam E. Seiber
        133   D. MacAdam
        135   R. Wilson, D. MacAdam, D. MacAdam
        137   R. Wilson, D. MacAdam
        141-181   J.-L. Grondin

Index

Page numbers in italics refer to illustrations; page numbers followed by "n" refer to captions.